CONTENTS

FOREWORD 1990

Theories of education abound. Dewey, Kilpatrick, Hutchins, and Adler started the dialogue in the early years. More recently, Skinner, Piaget, Illich, Hirsch and Bloom have spoken. Throughout the twentieth century, they and many others have all had their say, articulating a library of ideas rich in insight and promise. Over the decades, educational strategies have piled up, and scholars now find themselves with a too full bag of competing doctrines by which to organize and operate the American educational industry. We cannot seem to agree among ourselves on the central purpose of schooling.

Some theories are subject-centered, the curriculum holding the high ground. Others are problem-oriented, the student moving from passive to active participant in the act of learning. Yet others are behavioristic, relying on overt incentives to engender clear thought and right conduct. A few call for dismantling schools altogether and returning to apprenticeship on a massive scale.

What is conspicuously absent from the pantheon of educational strategies is one which focuses on and celebrates the personal self, the individual growing into his or her singular, idiosyncratic place in the world. This book addresses that possibility.

As a focused treatment of a particular position, this volume can be used as a supplement to several different approaches to the study of teaching and learning: In an introduction to education, the book provides a brief but thorough understanding of an educational point of view not customarily covered in such courses. In a survey on educational psychology, this book can supplement the study of deterministic behaviorism by offering a humanistic counter argument that the human being is more than a reinforceable organism. In a course on educational philosophy, the present volume can fill out the study of Essentialism and Progressivism by articulating a radical position on learner-centered pedagogical strategies.

For the general reader, this small volume may offer a window on unfamiliar but arresting scenery. The philosophy of Existentialism differs from other points of view in a critical way: It makes one think about human options. It directs one's attention to the importance of becoming the sole author of one's own life. As such, the argument can arouse as well as soothe.

The book was first published in 1966 as one of a series of paperbacks on several philosophical positions — Idealism, Realism, Pragmatism, and Existentialism. In its present form, it is virtually unchanged from the original. Unarguably, much has happened in the modern world over the last couple of decades, but Existentialism still survives as a viable philosophy of life and education. Its message is still as fresh and straightforward and commanding as it was a generation ago.

Following this Foreword is the Preface to the original edition. I wish to reiterate my gratitude to those mentioned in the final paragraph for their help in preparing the original manuscript. In addition, may I thank Catherine Fishel Morris for her continuing support in offering thoughtful critiques of my writing and in helping me make my ideas clear.

Van Cleve Morris

Wilmette, Illinois
January, 1990

EXISTENTIALISM IN EDUCATION

EXISTENTIALISM IN EDUCATION

what it means

VAN CLEVE MORRIS

University of Illinois at Chicago

WAVELAND

PRESS, INC.

Prospect Heights, Illinois

For information about this book, write or call:

Waveland Press, Inc.
P.O. Box 400
Prospect Heights, Illinois 60070
(708) 634-0081

PREFACE 1966

In the fall of 1953, I found myself at Harvard University, sojourning as a post-doctoral Fellow under the generous patronage of the Fund for the Advancement of Education. The year's sabbatical was to be devoted to the study of comparative educational philosophy, and I had decided to start my work in Cambridge. It was during those stimulating months that I was introduced to Existentialist thought by Professor Robert Ulich.

Like most people, I was at first puzzled by this new point of view, unable to get the hang of a philosophy so sharply on edge to the familiar terrain of Dewey's Experimentalism which, by then, seemed to me so obviously right that I saw no need to look further for a general outlook on which to base my life and work. But first impressions are sometimes misleading. Certainly they were in this case, for I was soon to feel a strange exhilaration in this novel view of man and his situation in the world. I knew then that this excitement would someday carry forward to an attempt to write an Existentialist theory of education.

The idea for this volume has been maturing in my mind for a good many years. Summers and vacations—on one occasion with the assistance of the Rutgers University Research Council—have been used for study and reflection. Now, at long last, the invitation from Harper & Row has met with my growing impatience to start writing, and the promise I made to myself to do this book has been kept.

No one writes a book without realizing how far short it falls from what he wanted it to be. All a dogged author can do is to hedge his arrogance by asking others to criticize his work. Professor William Barrett, Department of Philosophy at New York University, supplied wise and critical comments on the handling of philosophical concepts. Professor Ernest Bayles, School of Education at the University of Kansas and Editor of this series, offered helpful suggestions on the treatment of educational theory. Professor Jacqueline Berke, Department of English at Drew University, served as my perceptive and demanding writing coach. Professor Sally Anthony, Department of Education at San Diego State College, reacted to the manuscript in the role of a nonspecialist but interested professional educator. My wife, Eloise, once again exhibited her considerable skills as wielder of the blue pencil. Still others, colleagues and friends too numerous to mention, gave me helpful advice—sometimes almost more than I really wanted. Mrs. Edythe Randall, amanuensis supreme, prepared the manuscript.

To these individuals I extend an author's gratitude. If I did not accept all of their suggestions, they and I know that when all of the advice is in, it is the author who must decide what to say and how to say it. This means that they are relieved of responsibility for the way things have turned out. The book is mine, and I will answer for it.

Van Cleve Morris

EXISTENTIALISM IN EDUCATION

PROLOGUE

Existentialism is a theory of individual meaning. It asks each person to ponder the reason for his existing.

As philosophies go, Existentialism may be said to be something of a "special case." Voiced a century ago by a tormented man, then ignored by an age of reason, suddenly springing to life out of the rubble of tragedy and crisis, Existentialism would seem to be a philosophy fit only for persons and worlds gone mad. As a view of life, its career so far offers only the most questionable of credentials.

Søren Kierkegaard, the Danish theologian of the early 1800s generally regarded as the first major Existential thinker, was a man beset by public scorn and personal heartbreak. As a philosopher, he was an iconoclast in the classic tradition, trying, among other things, to erase the pretty diagrams which the Hegelians had chalked on the European conscience. In a stream of monologues

1

and diary entries, published under thinly veiled and not very cryptic pseudonyms, he ridiculed the Grand Designs of the "system builders," preferring instead to record the struggle of a single individual questioning the meaning of his own existence.

The nineteenth century paid little attention to Kierkegaard. At least in the West, men were preoccupied with proving out the big systems by seeking truth in the outside world. Nobody was interested in the prattlings of a man searching for truth within himself. And it did seem, at the time, that the search for objective, scientific truth was indeed the right pursuit. For science *did* produce knowledge; it did, indeed, rationalize experience.

By the twentieth century, however, the Grand Designs began to collapse; like cardboard boxes in the rain, they quietly folded into grotesque shapes of irrelevance. Science, having promised so much, had not delivered. As a logic for explaining the world, it seemed helpless before the juggernaut of modern events. How, one might ask, can science and system rationalize an age in which men schedule two world wars in every lifetime and casually discuss, as just another problem in social affairs, the prospect of total human annihilation?

In this unlikely environment, Existential thought has finally found a place to speak. Becoming articulate especially in war-rent, post-Occupation France and in spent and beaten Germany, Existentialism has spoken the troubled thoughts of the bewildered, "cornered" European people. In drama and fiction, as well as technical philosophy, such writers as Martin Heidegger, Karl Jaspers, Gabriel Marcel, Albert Camus, and Jean-Paul Sartre have addressed the West's attention once again to Kierkegaard's question.

It is said that Existentialism is a philosophy of crisis, a theory of life and man particularly suited to our anxious time. But this can be understood two ways. If it means that Existentialism is the spiritual medicine which can quiet man's nerves and steady him for living in an age of peril, then it is certainly false. Existentialism is no analgesic. If Existentialism is a philosophy of crisis, let this be understood to mean that it is a *feature of* the crisis rather than a *shield against* it.

This is not, it must be said, a very promising note to sound. It explains, I suppose, why Existentialism's reception beyond the Continent has been so unenthusiastic. Imported into the United States over the past couple of decades, Existentialism has had to buck not only the happy insouciance of a fun-geared, thing-ridden society but also the more sophisticated notion that the experimental sciences and the positive logics have taken us philosophically as far as we can go, and that further discussion of the meaning of man in the world is useless and silly.

Existentialism therefore enjoys only the most precarious of reputations today. Many people, even intellectuals who presumably should know better, have the vague feeling that it is a new and somewhat illicit poetry concocted in a nihilist atmosphere on the Parisian Left Bank by intense characters who wear little beards. Some of our national magazines have depicted it as a movement of the Big No, the strident dogma of the beatniks, who have merely made a convention of negation and who parade their negativisms, in dirty sweat shirts and stringy hair, before the tourists in the coffeehouses of Greenwich Village and North Beach. Some people feel even more strongly about it, registering agreement with the Italian philosopher Guido de Ruggiero, who calls Existentialism "metaphysical pornography."

Yes, the credentials are dubious, the reactions unflattering.

It is difficult to counter this impression. But, strangly enough, the Existentialists feel no urgency to do so. Existentialism is not a missionary movement. It does not promise anything. Rather, it tells us what is at stake in the task of being human. Its one claim to our attention is its shattering candor, betokened in its starting ground rule: There is a real possibility that we live in a meaningless world. Are we, it asks, equal to the task of living in such a world?

Most people, Americans in particular, find this difficult to listen to. It gives them a spiritual headache, a dizziness of the metaphysic. They are disenchanted by a philosophy which seems so bleak, which declines to offer reassurance that man has a reason for being and that the universe is somehow "on our side."

This reaction can possibly be traced to places deep within the American psyche. It must be remembered that the American people, not discounting what individuals and minority groups may encounter, have never really known the meaning of tragedy. Spared the crunching boot and the 2:00 A.M. doorknock, lacking experience with violence and holocaust, twentieth-century style, never having known the feeling of the constant fear of death, the American people cannot be expected to share the mood and temper of those in other parts of the world for whom mere survival has become a deliberate daily project. This is, I suggest, the real significance of the word "tragedy"—not simply defeat and grief, but the pain of having to struggle to establish and certify one's own significance in the world. In this sense, the American people have not yet developed, in Unamuno's phrase, the tragic sense of life.

Americans approach Existentialism the way they approach an automobile accident or a train wreck—slowing down their own vehicle, stepping out, edging forward, repelled at the sight they see, yet attracted and pressing toward the vortex of suffering, peering over shoulders lest they miss something even more bizarre and gruesome, finally retreating like spectators from a stadium. And they will most certainly devour—to the very last paragraph—next morning's newspaper accounts of the smashup. At arm's length almost anything is mentally digestible!

So with this philosophy. A kind of intellectual train wreck, it has attracted a gallery of track-side curiosity seekers. If you, the reader, are in the gallery, may I greet you. At least you are not home reading the newspaper. And don't be in a hurry to leave. For here, at the scene of the crash, is where we can best carry on our dialogue. It is only when men are in the presence of extremity that they can best talk about the meaning of life. This is what Existentialism proposes to do: examine the meaning of human life.

As such, it is the kind of philosophy which addresses each one of us—you, the reader, and me, the author—in the most personal of ways. It asks us to ask ourselves what significance we can attach to our own presence in the world. This is a sobering assignment, and quite probably an unpleasant one, too. Yet, for all its unpleasantness, it is a task we seem unable to turn from. We are chained to this puzzle, the meaning of our own existing. And the surprise is that, as study continues and awareness grows, the unpleasantness slowly turns to a new and somehow deeper sense of what it means to be a man. If Existentialism must begin in agony, it is capable of issuing in exhilarating sensations of human power. It is these affirmative thrusts of the philosophy which have been too much overlooked and which shall therefore be accentuated in this discussion.

Because Existentialism asks the kinds of questions it does, its rhetoric differs from that of other philosophies:

Existentialism is more interested in particulars than in universals. It is more interested in trying to fathom the import of a single human life than in coming to some grand category which allegedly explains the "All" and the "One."

It discusses the subjective. And since the subjective is, in a manner of speaking, undiscussable, there is need to invoke the services of metaphor, allegory, and symbol.

It discusses the individual. Our response to it, yours and mine, is likely to be personal. Hence the conversational tone of this book.

One may reasonably ask just what the prospects are for a theory of education to come out of this unorthodox set of ideas. There *are* difficulties—admittedly. We are, for one thing, working from a very small library, a bookshelf maybe not even two feet long. Few Existentialist writers have taken up questions in what we have come to call the social sciences. Even fewer have ventured into a discussion of education. For another thing, and perhaps more decisive, in the field of philosophy we continue to work these days in the rigorous and unyielding climate of Anglo-American Positivism, a movement dedicated to the analysis of logic and language. Existentialism does not flourish in such a climate; the air is too heavy with p's and q's. Under analysis, Existentialist prose gets lost in a thicket of equations. But what is more disturbing is the Positivist contention that no prescriptions—for education or anything else—can logically be drawn from any philosophical position, including Existentialism. From an "is" there issues no "ought." What this dictum has to mean is that, logically speaking, philosophy is useless as a guide to conduct. Since this principle presumably applies to the philosophy of Positivism also, it would appear to be self-canceling. At any rate, I have chosen to ignore it.

In the face of these deterrents, I offer Part Two as a possible Existential theory of education. There, we undertake a development of the theory itself and an examination of the derivative pedagogy. But before that we must come to feel the intense directness of Existentialist ideas. To this, in Part One, we now turn.

part one Existentialism as a philosophy

1

PARADOX AND THE EXISTENTIAL ENCOUNTER

THE EXISTENTIAL MOOD

Philosophies, like people, have temperaments. They seem to exhibit particular moods or "attitude sets" toward the world. In the case of Existentialism, this mood is very important for the understanding of its main ideas and is worth some comment.

Philosophy, as a pursuit, is now about 2500 years old. As one studies this long stretch of intellectual development, a peculiar trait of the philosophical mind reveals itself: the steady persistence of the unspoken assumption that the universe, whatever it is, is built

9

along lines that are consistent with the strivings and purposes of man. As noted in the Prologue, the convention in philosophy has been to take for granted that the universe is a friendly arena of our endeavors, that it is a "home" to man, and that man is not deluded when he thinks that he truly belongs here, that he is not an alien in this "country." From the pre-Socratics, with their conceptions of essence and quintessence, through Plato, Aristotle, Aquinas, and Hegel, there runs the current of assurance that the cosmos not only has a place for man but indeed requires and cherishes his presence. Man is both necessary and wanted in this place.

With the onset of the modern, empirical philosophies in the nineteenth and twentieth centuries, this sense of assurance may appear to have diminished. But actually all that has happened is a displacement of the warrant for the assurance, a shift from our trust in the big metaphysical systems of the traditional philosophers to a trust in the intricate epistemologies and logics of the empiricists. Now we are told that, if man cannot find safety in a metaphysical system, he may find it in an intellectual method. Man, it is announced, has the obligation to be intelligent, and he can signify his consent to this obligation by putting himself in the hands of a certain logic and regulating his thought according to definite and specific rules.

Thus does the "safety syndrome" reappear. Positive thinking is the new imperium; logic takes the place of metaphysics as our guard against alienation. Man is given a new, and presumably better, reason for believing that he belongs in the world and has a meaningful job to do. We feel "at home" in a world in which "the obligation to be intelligent" is the ultimate unarguable principle and a preordered, precertified logic awaits to teach us how to be intelligent and how to get to the truth. The truths we reach are admittedly tentative and corrigible, but the logic itself is positive and certain. It is in the logic that we now find peace and comfort. The "thinking man" is the new paradigm, and we can all aspire to be like him if we will only keep careful check on our thought processes.

As you might expect, Existentialism rejects the above thesis. If one wishes to place his faith in a logic instead of a metaphysic, the Existentialist might say, that is understandable. But let this be clearly seen as a *faith* and nothing more. There is no necessity or compelling obligation that says I must believe in logic, as one might believe in God, before I can be considered properly serious about the problems of men. It's like being given a test of mental competence—if you don't pass, nobody is obliged to listen to what you say. But who says that the "obligation to be intelligent" is unarguable? More important, who says that there is only one, positive, logical way to be "intelligent" in this world?

In the raising of such questions, Existentialism approaches the philosophical enterprise with a certain disdain of the empirical philosophies. It brings to work every morning an honest doubt as to whether any particular faith—in a metaphysic, in a logic, in whatever—can ever be fully certified. Is any faith, it asks, really unarguable? Is faith in logic and reason something we automatically owe to the world? Is it the only appropriate response men can make to their world? Indeed, is the world the kind of place in which the phrase "human response" has any meaning? Maybe the world isn't listening. And if it isn't, how are we ever to know that we have "said" the right thing?

The mood of Existentialism is implicit in all of these questions. It is a mood of wishing to reopen the question as to whether the universe is friendly to man, without the predisposition of believing the answer will always turn out to be "Yes." Other answers are just as possible.

Once one acknowledges this philosophical mood and works within it, he can begin to see that some of our understandings about men and the world do not come to us from metaphysics or logic; they come to us from ourselves. They are known somehow internally without the assistance of any intellectual formulas or propositional grammars. It is these understandings with which Existentialism starts. Three of them

> Human subjectivity
> Paradox
> Anxiety

generate all Existential thinking and therefore require special attention.

HUMAN SUBJECTIVITY

Existentialism's very name suggests the central importance of the word "exist." Unfortunately, it is not an easy word to understand, despite its frequent appearance in everyday talk. One pathway into its meaning is through the private, subjective awareness we each have of our own selves as existing in the world.

The first thing to exist is me.[1] This may be ungrammatical and seemingly arrogant, but it is the best way to plunge to the heart of the seminal existential concept. What it means is this: All philosophizing begins with an existing being aware of his own existing. Every thought he thinks, every word he places on paper, every act he commits, derives *its* existence from *his* prior existing.

One of the ridiculous puzzles of philosophy has been the question: Do I really exist? It is ridiculous because it is not a problem; no philosopher genuinely doubted his own existence. And we must certainly include in this generalization Descartes himself. Descartes' logic seemed to be impeccable, and he appeared to be really sincere in trying to prove his own existence. But his argument was deceptive, flawed by a subtle error:

Descartes wanted to develop an argument to support the contention "I am." In approaching this problem, he decided to begin by wiping the slate clean and doubting the existence of everything, including himself. What he could not doubt the existence of, however, was his own doubting. So he came up with the classic "*Cogito, ergo sum*" ("I think, therefore I am"). But it is obvious even to an untrained mind that in uttering the first "I" Descartes had already assumed his conclusion "I am." What is the sense, therefore, of going through this solemn syllogism only to find at the end of it a "startling truth" that you have already uttered by the very first sound your lips have made? To think that centuries of philosophy have been bewitched by the *Cogito!*

Some philosophers have tried to save Descartes by insisting that what he really meant by the *Cogito* was not "I think" but rather something like "Thinking is going on here." This turns out to be even more precarious. For in the formulation "Thinking is going on here, therefore, I exist" we have uttered a *non sequitur* of the most outrageous sort. Nothing existential follows from the remark "Thinking is going on here." All that follows is the question: Who is speaking? We are driven back inevitably to the first Cartesian "I."

The "I" comes first. I am the first existent, "the first thing that is." The utterance "I exist" must necessarily precede any other sentence I wish to say.[2] "In the beginning was the Word, and the Word was the pronoun 'I.'" All else must wait upon this.

The priority of the existential "I" is therefore a starting hypothesis. It is a hypothesis only, since there is no conceivable way to verify it. But, as hypothesis, it arouses no doubt or skepticism. Of all the propositions I can utter, the assertion "I am" is by all measure the one of which I am most certain.

The hypothesis is central to all forms of Existentialism and may be generalized with the dictum: "Existence precedes essence." What this phrase means is that the *fact* of my existing is antecedent to any other fact or any other understanding I may have of the world, including the understanding of my own essence. Likewise, the *fact* of man's presence in the world is antecedent to any other fact that may be uttered about the world.

By way of analogy, we may say that in the micro-world, in our everyday world of producing and consuming, it is sensible to believe that essence precedes existence. That is to say, the plan of a table must be in the carpenter's mind before he builds the table; the design of the Cadillac must be in the minds of the engineers at General Motors before the Cadillac is actually brought into existence. This is plain enough. But in the macro-world, where man himself appears to be the "product" of some higher artificer, the sequence "essence first, existence second" does not hold, for whatever design or essence he may assert as being prior to his own existence is necessarily of his own creation. One cannot ask the question: What did God have in mind when he created man? without realizing that any answer must issue from man's own lips. Man is therefore in the odd position of being his own designer or essence-giver. And, we may ask, what is the essence of a being who creates his own essence? The answer must be that this is always an open question, to be answered by every individual in the process of living his life and thereby giving meaning and essence to his existence.

And here is just the point: this being, man, exists first. How else could he ask himself all these questions? He first *is*; then he asks himself *what* he is. One can see therefore that Existentialism gets its name from its insistence that existing comes first; my existing—personal, individual, a subjective awareness that is nevertheless certain—is the absolutely raw datum of the world. I have simply "turned up" in existence, simply appeared on the scene. In the metaphor of some Existentialists, I have been "thrown" into existence, whence I know not. I become aware of, I wake up to, my existing. This is the dawn of consciousness: consciousness becoming aware of itself as present in the world.

Now, it is possible that the above may be construed as a foolish solipsism, as if the Existentialist were saying, "I am all that there is." Note, however, that he is making no such assertion. He is saying only, "I must assume my own existence as a fact before I may reflect upon the existence of other occupants of the world." As Martin Buber has put it, "This does not mean that nothing exists except [man]. But all else lives in *his* light."[3] And it should be clearly understood that this covers the past as well as the present. In order to consider the question of Caesar's existence in history, I must necessarily assume my own existence as a condition for considering it. In that sense, then, I may be said to be existentially prior to Caesar.

The point is that the ground of all reflection is human subjectivity, the awareness of personal existing. It is from this subjective base that all intellectual expeditions must start out. Such being the case, all pronouncements about the meaning of life—and that is what philosophy claims to teach us—originate in and therefore bear some relation to the meanings we individually find in our own lives. Neither philosophy nor any other human endeavor can plumb deeper or rise higher than what man can say about himself, personally, in the predicament of existing.

We may properly call it a "predicament" because awareness of the priority of the "I" fans out to other awarenesses with which we find ourselves not completely able to cope. One of these is what we may designate as the awareness of paradox, the second of Existentialism's basic understandings.

PARADOX

Paradox consists in holding two contrary views of the significance of our own existing. One of these views may be explained in the following way: When I[4] awake to the fact of my existing, when I recognize the absolute priority of the pronoun "I" in the structure of my life and world, I am struck by the fact that this "I" that I know seems to be the only one of its kind in existence. There is an absolute uniqueness of the phenomenon of my own selfhood. I peer out on the world with all its apparent order and system. It seems to contain a multi-variety of items, all of them understood under their own rubrics and categories, like the items in a Sears, Roebuck catalog. Yet, I know that I am really different from all else I behold there. I am not to be found under any of the rubrics. I am not in the catalog; there is no entry for me in the index; the world apparently "does not carry that item." The reason is that there are no rubrics under which I could be classified. Or, better, *I am my own rubric*, the only instance of this item in existence, a singular phenomenon never to be repeated. Never again this particular arrangement of protoplasmic molecules, never again this particular origin or history, never again this particular set of traits and attitudes. Never again shall another Van Cleve Morris come into the world.[5] What am I to make of this uniqueness, this one-and-only-oneness? Do not most of us translate it into a positive quality, a basic value, a characteristic to be glad of? To be one of a kind, to be a single instance, is to be a phenomenon worthy of attention in the world.

There is an irony to the fact that most religions and philosophies and some political theories, most notably Western democracy, have made so much of the uniqueness of the individual and the sanctity of the person. We are reminded, over and over again, of Kant's imperative that each man is to be treated as end, never as means. And the American ethic, from Jefferson to the present, has reiterated the injunction that each person is precious, the individual

always superior to the state. The irony is that we already *know* it!
No one has to convince us of the truth of this principle. It is somehow known and believed by each one of us even before anyone
says it.

Sometimes the most prosaic of metaphors helps to illuminate
our attempt to convey profound ideas. For example, we often remark in commenting on an unusual friend or acquaintance, "Yes,
he's quite a person. They threw away the mold when they made
that fellow!" Doesn't everyone think of himself in terms of this
metaphor?

No matter what happens, I shall always insist that my own existing, my being an "instance" of man, is an unrepeatable datum in
the world. Furthermore, I am permanent, a datum written with
indelible ink into the cosmic ledger book, never to be erased or
expunged. It may be in very small print, but it is there forever. I
assign to myself, therefore—without any assistance from Christian
doctrine or democratic preachments—an absolute value and an ultimate worth. I count, I matter in the scheme of things. My existing makes a difference; the cosmos wouldn't be quite the same
without me.

This is one side of Existential paradox. The other side: My existence is a big joke, a huge delusion! Each of us recognizes, when
we reflect on it for a moment, that we count for absolutely nothing.
The cosmos does not require our presence. Not in the slightest.
Look around you—funerals every day! And what does it matter?
Isn't the loss made up somehow, by putting others in the vacated
places?

If I were to fall into the Chicago Drainage Canal, which flows
near Chicago Circle, and wash down the Mississippi River into
the Gulf, what difference would it make? There would, I presume,
be some stir. The University community would be jostled, ever so
slightly; there would necessarily be a reassignment of my responsi-
bilities to others until a replacement could be found. (One can
always hope that the flag might fly at half-staff for a day or so.)
Certainly my loved ones, those close to me, would grieve, and there
would be concentric circles of sorrow extending outward among
them. But the intensity of the sorrow would decrease "by the square

of the distance"; by the time it reached my last cousin, it would have faded into nothing.

Sooner or later, the loss would be forgotten. My friends would put it out of mind and return to work. The University would run the flag back up the flagpole and would find a replacement—because I *am* replaceable. And my family and relations would adjust to a world without me. In time, all would heal over, and my "I," the content of my selfhood, would be lost, expunged from existence. The ideas I had expressed would be forgotten; the words I wrote would molder in the libraries. Eventually all would go "down the drain." And men living a hundred or five hundred years from now would have no inkling that I had been here.

So, I will eventually be erased from the universe. I do not particularly like to think about it, but I must recognize this truth. In the end, the significance of my presence in the world will inevitably reduce to that absolute zero usually reserved for Centigrade thermometers at $-273.16°$, where all molecular movement has to come to a stop. That will be the situation: In ten, or a hundred, or five hundred years, all residual effects of my existence shall have disappeared, all "motions" shall have expended their last quantum of energy, and the fact of my presence, while still a fact, shall have been emptied of significance, my meaning in the world finally exhausted and spent.

This, then, is the paradox, and every man must live with it. It is to know two things about oneself: (1) that one is of absolute value in the world, and (2) that one is of absolutely no value whatsoever. These two truths are contradictory, but they are both true. It may be that they are known to an individual in different ways; perhaps my subjectivity tells me the first and my empirical reason tells me the second. But that is beside the point. I believe them both, and at once.

Now, it appears that, of the two, the former seems the hardier, the sturdier view, the more difficult to put down. It keeps growing through the cracks in the concrete wall of purely rational, empirical truth. If for no other reason than its attractiveness, the notion that one really counts for something in the world wins the greater attention. We try not to think about the second possibility too much;

it is too depressing. And yet it haunts us as being quite as possible an outcome as the former. It pricks and taunts. It whispers that we are living a Great Big Joke!

But our subjectivity is oblivious. We turn aside the whisper. We give no answer because the suggestion is outrageous, and we cannot entertain it seriously. We address ourselves instead to the former possibility, sensing a kind of determination in ourselves to see to it that this alternative must somehow be made to emerge as the correct answer to the paradox.

The awareness of existence

The paradox itself originates in a peculiar facility of *homo sapiens,* apparently not shared by other entities in the world, namely, awareness of existence as such. Sartre once remarked that "man is the being by whom nothingness comes into the world." This is quite correct, and we shall examine it in a moment, but first an antecedent axiom should be stated: "Man is the being by whom existence itself comes into being." If this seems redundant or tautological, we can nevertheless extract some meaning from it, namely, that the notion of existence is "man-made." The word "existence" and its equivalents (e.g., "being," "to be," "to exist") enjoy no higher rank in the English language than any other word, say, "apple" or "vertical" or "jump." Like all the rest, it is a symbol which we employ in describing our experience; language itself is nothing more than the invention, the organization, and the conventional use of symbols. And since man is the originator of language, he must be thought of as the originator of the notion of existence or being.

This is not to say that man is the creator of whatever exists. Rather, he is the creator of the *existence-idea;* he is the first to be aware of existence and to give it a name. He is the being to whom the notion of existence first occurs. In an Existential account of paleohistory, it could be said that what we call *man* did not appear until he became aware of the *existence-idea.* Not until *the awareness of existence* had been had[6] by some "agent" could such an agent have been classified, in retrospect, as *human.* Hence, the emergence of this awareness-of-existence and the emergence of man may be thought of as simultaneous. One might say that man is the occasion for the emergence of the awareness, and that the awareness is the occasion for the emergence of man. Without man, the awareness would have no footing. "Man" and "awareness of existence" are equivalent terms; we mean by "man" a being aware of being.

Now, if man is the "initiating vehicle" for the existence-idea— its "author," so to speak—he finds himself in the unusual circumstance of having to decide whether to assign this "man-made" characteristic to or withhold it from the phenomena he finds in his experience. He assigns it (the idea of "existence") most readily, we have seen, to the phenomenon of his own self; there seems to be little question about this. But with what certainty the characteristic of "existence" can be assigned to other phenomena man is not sure.

The difficulty lies in the fact that the concept itself, though originating in man's own awareness, cannot be defined by its "author." The reason is evident:

Every definition is the determination of a concept by indicating its higher genus and the differentia specifica. But since being is itself the supreme genus, it is evidently impossible to find a higher genus in which it would be included; therefore any definition of being becomes logically impossible.[7]

But note: this lack of definition does not deter man in the slightest from assigning the characteristic of "existence" to his own selfhood. It is only when the question comes up of the existence of phenomena beyond his own skin that the lack of a definition emerges as troublesome.

This may explain the difficulty that philosophy has had with metaphysics for so many centuries. Man is the author of the *existence-idea*. He is therefore put in the situation of being its "dispenser" in the world. But he cannot dispense it with a sure and steady hand because he cannot seem to determine the criteria for dispensation. If he says, "X exists; Y does not," how is he certain that the verb will hold? The wreckage and clutter of two millennia of metaphysics and ontology attest to his doubt.

But there is no doubt about one's own existing. This is the metaphysics without flaw. Definition or no, I exist. If I cannot *know* it rationally through a definition, I can *feel* it. I do not need a definition to comprehend what it means in my case. I simply emerged into a state of awareness of my own existing. I do not need to be convinced of this. I am the being by whom the awareness of my existence came into being. And I have a monopoly on this particular awareness. It is absolutely private and mine.

The awareness of nothingness

We said a moment ago that the paradox originated in man's awareness of existence as such. This is not entirely accurate. If man could be aware only of existence, there would be no paradox. The paradox stems from the fact that no awareness can be had of existence without a coordinate awareness of nonexistence. It is because these two awarenesses must always go together that the paradox arises.

As we have seen, man cannot seem to define the infinitive "to be," because "being" cannot be included in any "higher genus." Some philosophers have not taken such disability too seriously; they believe that the "higher genus" we are looking for is *nothingness* or *nonbeing*. This, they contend, is the background against which we may get a glimpse of being. The trouble is that, in order to establish nothingness as a background, we must somehow assign to it the characteristic of existence, and to do so would be equivalent to saying that nothingness is a somethingness, or that nonbeing is a special case of being. But then we are back in our old difficulty. How is it possible to understand being as included in the "higher genus" of nonbeing, when nonbeing is defined as a subclass of being? This approach quite obviously will not do.

Perhaps what is necessary right here is to back away from our problem temporarily to get another look at it. If "being" is undefinable, let it remain. If we understand the word—and we do understand it—isn't that enough? Perhaps all understandings that come to us via our subjectivities are essentially undefinable, in a strict, cognitive sense of that term. But their stature as understandings is not diminished thereby. Try, for instance, to define the word "time." An impossibility! And yet, for all its cognitive density, "time" still means something understandable.

By relieving ourselves of the obligation to define "being," we skirt the embarrassment of concocting some odd logic by which nothingness is made into a something. But there is a danger that, in avoiding embarrassment, we retreat to the equally profitless position of saying that the term "nothingness" must be ruled out altogether. It simply cannot be ruled out. It *does* play a role. The awareness of nothingness can be quite as vivid as the awareness of being, and this awareness, it turns out, lies at the root of the ultimate questions we have about life.

The terms "being" and "nothingness" are not some kind of special, esoteric argot of philosophers. On the contrary, they are to be understood in their everyday sense. We live in a world of existing things; we say that chairs exist, houses exist, men exist, trees exist. And obviously it is possible to conceive of the nonexistence of any one of these. Now, suppose we were simply to generalize our conception to imagine the nonexistence of everything that we conceive of as existing. Would not this be a situation of nothingness, extending in all "directions"? Space would be gone; time would be gone, human thought would be gone; God would be gone.

A time will come when this Universe and Nature itself will be extinguished. And just as of the grandest kingdoms and empires of mankind and the marvellous things achieved therein, very famous in their own time, no vestige or memory remains to-day, so, in like manner, of the entire world there will remain not a single trace, but a naked silence and a most profound stillness will fill the immensity of space. And so before ever it has been uttered or understood, this admirable and fearful secret of universal existence will be obliterated and lost.[8]

I suppose we might ask, Why "admirable"? Is it *good* that the universe exists? It is because men invariably answer this question in the affirmative that nothingness seems to them such a tragedy. It would be a shame, we think, for all to come literally to naught. As Unamuno says, nothingness is something we should fight against.

But, to return to the argument, where did this notion of nothingness come from in the first place? It came, actually, from the same source as the notion of being, i.e., from man's awareness. If we can conceive of chairs or worlds existing, how can we conceive of chairs no longer existing? It must be because we, in our existential awareness, have brought with us this power to annihilate, to negate. We let into our awareness of existence the "foreign substance" of nothingness because without the irritation of the foreign substance the awareness itself would have no density; it would not be an awareness. And this is a basic proposition: To understand what it means for something "to be" is to understand what it means for that thing "not to be."

Sartre speaks of nothingness as "coiled in the heart of being—like a worm." I would suggest another metaphor. In northern Michigan, a bird will take a nip out of an unripened sweet cherry. The ripening process will leave a scar, but the cherry's "response" to the injury is invariably to become more succulent. The cherry's wound is the sign of higher quality. Cherries, after all, are to be eaten, not looked at. Nothingness is a wound in being, but precisely because of the wound, being becomes intensified in our awareness. Being, after all, is to be understood, not merely wondered at.

In this connection the doughnut metaphor, trivial as it is, may be instructive. Nothingness is the hole. Of course, without the doughnut, no hole. But keep in mind that without the hole, no doughnut.[9]

The point is that we do not need to turn "nothingness" into a something in order to legitimize it in our discourse. Nor is it necessary, in technical ontology, to conceive of nothingness as *"outside of* being, [or] as a complementary, abstract notion [as Hegel thought, or] as an infinite milieu where being is suspended."[10] Rather, nothingness is "at the heart of Being"[11] because it is brought in by the very agent who has established being, i.e., man. Man, then, is the being by whom the nothingness-idea comes into the world. As the bearer of these two awarenesses, he is the "center of the universe" in the sense that he is the center of existence and negation.

Rarefied as it may seem, this talk about being and nothingness does not refer to some stratospheric platform of human thought processes accessible only to philosophers. The element of nothingness, in the above sense, appears in the most prosaic of circumstances. To use one of Sartre's oft-cited allegories, suppose that I call up my friend Pierre and ask him to meet me at Josette's Café in a half-hour. I show up at the appointed time and find Pierre not there. Now, is it not the case that a quality has been introduced into the phenomenal situation by myself which the ontological situation does not, by itself, possess? That is to say, the quality of Pierre-not-being-there is a constituent part of the awareness I have of the café. His absence is a concrete aspect of the phenomenon unfolding before my eyes. And I am the occasion for this concrete aspect's appearing, for without my awareness, Pierre-not-being-there is a wholly different matter from Wellington-not-being-in-the-café. I am not expecting Wellington; his absence does not enter the phenomenal situation, and on *my* account—since I am the agent by whom absences and not-being-there's take on concreteness. I am the "author" of nothingness. I am responsible for there being nothingnesses in the world.

ANXIETY

A few pages back, it was pointed out that we could conceive of the nothingness of chairs and worlds. And we have seen in the section just above that we are able not only to *conceive* of nothingnesses but actually to *experience* them—indeed, to become the very vehicle for their emergence. However, in all of these illustrations, we have been considering the existence or nonexistence of phenomena beyond our own skin. Can we as easily open up for consideration the existence or nonexistence of our own selves?

The question is ridiculous on its face. Of course not! I can stand aside and speak in a very scholarly way about the being or nonbeing of chairs or Pierres. I can conceive of them and deliberately experience them as absent from the world. I can even dare to speak of the nonbeing of the world itself, so long as I maintain a safe distance—so long, that is, as I don't include myself. But if I am *in* the world, and if the world could pass into nonbeing, then obviously I would have to go. And this prospect, different in kind from the others, simply cannot be contemplated in the same mood or spirit.

Why not? The reason is this: If I am in no doubt whatsoever about assigning the characteristic of "existence" to my own selfhood, then "nothingness" must be absolutely excluded from consideration; it cannot be entertained as an option. My awareness of my own existence is, shall we say, "puncture proof." However, although I seem to be absolutely invulnerable to all suggestions that I do not exist, I am absolutely defenseless against the suggestion that some day I might not exist. To recognize, in the certainty of one's own existence, that this existence need never have occurred or, equally, that this existence could pass away in a flicker and indeed may disappear eventually with no loss is to be overcome by an emotion of the most overpowering sort.

Heidegger raised the question "Why is there something instead of nothing; why is there anything at all?" And this is an agonizing question in its own right. But when it is rephrased to read, "Why am *I* at all?" the lack of a ready answer jars and scrambles all logic. The question has the effect of setting off a demolition of the entire content of a human subjectivity. Like a huge gravel pit in the middle of town, there appears an aching void, an aching nothingness at the heart of the spirit.

I recall a Protestant clergyman who once spoke before an undergraduate audience in connection with a "Religion in Life" week at a southern university. His Scottish accent was beguiling and his homiletics spectacular. His main contribution, however, lay in a very simple question. Revolving his huge right arm in a counterclockwise sweep, and letting his extended index finger eventually land, to synchronize with his gaze, upon an unsuspecting sophomore, he would inquire, "And what are *you* doing here?" He obviously did not mean ". . . in this lecture hall?" or ". . . in this university?" He meant, "What are you doing here, *in the world?*" "Just why are you cluttering up the existential landscape with your presence?"

It is an interesting question. It calls into play the most numbing of human feelings. What if I were to disappear, what if I were to be completely expunged, rubbed out, erased from existence with no trace? Even hell seems preferable. The numbing feeling, for better or worse, has been dubbed "anxiety." Anxiety, as Tillich defines it, is "the state in which a being is aware of its possible nonbeing."[12] The label itself may be misleading, and perhaps we should pause to consider it.

Anxiety, in this context, is not to be confused with Freudian or psychoneurotic anxiety. That form of the ailment, what we might speak of as the psychosocial form, concerns the low-order problem of being out of adjustment with one's social environment. A "nothingness" has crept in, to be sure, but it is a nothingness occasioned be warped rapport with one's fellow man, and as such is theoretically curable. If one is cut off from psychic communication with others, the anxiety thus engendered has a cause which is, in theory, capable of being located and identified. And the psychiatrist or psychoanalyst can undertake therapeutic measures aimed at identifying and removing the cause.

The situation is entirely different with what we are now calling existential anxiety. It is an anxiety of the most profound sort, signifying alienation not merely from one's fellow human beings but from the world, from the very ground of existence. This form of anxiety does not seem to have any identifiable cause. There is no specifiable "nothingness," if you will, which can be pointed to and of which it might be said, "Here, doctor, here is the difficulty." And hence, there appears to be no suitable therapy. The malady is a kind of *ultimate ache* for which conventional psychiatric medicine has no specific.

The insertion of "alienation" in the above commentary is deliberate. We speak of an alien literally as a person who is not, at the moment, at home in his own country. But, unlike a mere tourist, the alien realizes he is not at home but does not wish or is not allowed to return to his homeland; for one reason or another he has taken up residence in his new country with the intention of calling it home. Now, consider his situation. He recognizes that, as an alien, as an "official stranger," he is neither accepted nor rejected. His presence makes no difference, one way or the other; he is no bother to have around, but, on the other hand, he would not be missed. His departure, were it to take place, would go unnoticed; the community is totally indifferent. His acknowledgment of these conditions would certainly incline him, I think, to feel a certain unease. Not despair, necessarily, but the unease of not "feeling at home."

The anxiety here under examination is of the sort one might feel upon realizing that he is "not at home" in the world, that he is somehow an alien in an "adopted land." It is not the emotion of hysteria, or anything so spectacular, but just the dull ache of knowing that one's existence is of no significance, that one could depart unnoticed, and the cosmos and all its parts would be totally indifferent to such a leave-taking.

Robert Frost once defined "home" as "the place where . . . they have to take you in." Occasionally, of course, the definition does not hold, and we hear that someone has been actually turned away from his own home. We shudder at the chill, the bleakness of it. But this cannot possibly compare with the bleakness of alienation from existence itself. To be a political alien or to be "de-homed" is unfortunate, but there are remedies; one can go out and make friends or work hard to deserve acceptance. But existential alienation has no remedy; it is a "nothingness" one cannot contend with.

For this reason some Existentialists prefer the word "dread," or "anguish," rather than "anxiety," to describe the feeling. Dread is a kind of "awe-full" fear. But listen to Heidegger:

> *Dread differs absolutely from fear. We are always afraid of this or that definite thing, which theatens us in this or that definite way. "Fear of" is generally "fear about" something. Since fear has this characteristic limitation—"of" and "about"—the man who is afraid, the nervous man, is always bound by the thing he is afraid of or by the state in which he finds himself. In his efforts to save himself from this "something" he becomes uncertain in relation to other things; in fact, he "loses his bearings" generally.*
>
> *In dread no such confusion can occur. It would be truer to say that dread is pervaded by a peculiar kind of peace. And although dread is always "dread of" it is not dread of this or that. "Dread of" is always a dreadful feeling "about"—but not about this or that. The indefiniteness of what we dread is not just lack of definition: it represents the essential impossibility of defining the "what."*[13]

As Heidegger says later on, "dread reveals nothingness." Instead of the object's producing the ache, it is the ache itself which provides the occasion for the appearance of nothingness; dread somehow illuminates what nothingness would be like so far as one's own existence is concerned.

THE AFFIRMATION OF SELF

In most of our daily living, the sense of dread is pushed out to the perimeters of consciousness. We try not to think about it too much, precisely because we seem to have no remedy for it. For most people, what we have been talking about—the possible non-being of oneself—is obviously a phenomenon ordinarily associated with death. And, indeed, Heidegger has analyzed it from that standpoint.

But we sometimes fail to realize that death, and the dread attending it, is the means by which the true exultation of being human can be realized. The *encounter with nothingness*, seemingly so unpromising as a starting problem in philosophical discourse, is in fact the test we should be willing to take as a demonstration of our worth in the world. It is not nothingness but the *encounter* with nothingness which provides the vehicle for our humanness to exhibit itself. Man is the being to whom the privilege has been given of testing whether he can live with the haunt of nothingness in the very act of his existing. I find in one of Heidegger's more provocative interpreters, Arland Ussher, the key of what I am trying to say. "Man," he says, "is not more than the beast because he dies, but because he knows, and can live with the knowledge, that he is 'fastened to a dying animal.' "[14]

What is the significance of being "fastened to a dying"—a nothingness-bound—"animal"? To me it has every significance; I think there is no test which can possibly outrank this as a device for summoning the very finest and best from each man. As Tillich has phrased it, the test calls forth "the courage to be." And just what is the magnitude of this courage? It is such that we are asked to face up to nothingness without flinching, to make the encounter with nothingness as a military general "engages opposing forces," and to advance against nothingness with the assertions and affirmations of one's own being. Nothingness, after all, is not a foregone conclusion; it is only a *possibility*.

I have spoken earlier in this chapter of the Existentialist notion that "existence precedes essence." That discussion was intended to explain that, while our *existence* is not in question, our *essence* most certainly is. As his own essence-giver, man finds his essence an open-ended question; his essence is *up to him!* Now, some individuals cannot stand living out a life which is an open question. They do not want their essence, their "whatness" in the world, to be left up to them. They want someone to advise them how to act, what to believe, what to be.

Here, you see, is the greatest, the most inglorious default, namely, to encounter the nothingness represented by one's lack of essence and to interpret this lack as a kind of deformity to be corrected or made up for by others. It is precisely the opposite of a deformity! The lack is an *invitation to be*—an invitation to be something worth being, an invitation to fill up the nothingness with an essence that is worthy of existing and undeserving of being lost.

It is as if we had all been invited by a huge international philanthropic foundation to participate in a very interesting research project: determination of the essence of man. By virtue of the research problem itself, there would be no "director," as such, but rather we would all hold equal rank in the undertaking; we would all be "research assistants" contributing our ideas as we developed them. How would it be possible to turn down such an invitation? What more flattering offer could one imagine than to be asked to help create "the essence of man"?

Existentialism has acquired a bad name because it dares to dwell upon unpleasant subject matter: nothingness, anxiety, dread, anguish, absurdity. Happy people deflect all talk of such concerns. They do not wish to be bothered. Yet only when we are willing to be bothered by these ideas can we effectively turn them around to face in the direction of a positive program of human action and definition. If the lack of an essence signifies a nothingness at the heart of my being, it is precisely this awareness of the void that can summon me to live out a more meaningful life. A human life is a cherry pecked by a bird; it has been inflicted with nothingness. And it is the infliction itself which provides the occasion for a positive affirmation of my self as a being worthy of being.

In his discerning and poignant book *The Tragic Sense of Life*, Miguel de Unamuno has restated and amplified the ethical thesis of Sénancour, early nineteenth-century writer. It is an intense message that Sénancour speaks: "Man is perishable. That may be; but let us perish resisting, and if it is nothingness that awaits us," let us so act that that would be an unjust fate.[15]

This, after all the nausea has cleared away, is the overpowering theme of Existentialism: the project of living one's life in such a way as to be deserving of something better than nothingness and obliteration; to confront nothingness, to *deny* nothingness, by filling it up with a life that ought never to be lost or annihilated.

NOTES

1. When Fichte, the German philosopher, uttered a similar proposition, his friends are reported to have asked, "What does his wife think about this?"

2. The technically trained reader will possibly expect to find here some acknowledgment of Russell's Theory of Descriptions. Examination of this Theory as it relates to the problem of existence appears in Chapter 4 on p. 84.

3. Martin Buber, *I and Thou*, 2nd ed., trans. by R. G. Smith (New York: Charles Scribner's Sons, 1958), p. 8.

4. The use of the first person singular may be misleading here. I am speaking not only of myself but rather in behalf of myself and you, the reader. I believe you might express yourself similarly, given the opportunity. If I were to employ the term "we," someone might look upon it as the "editorial 'we' " which, of course, it is not. I use the first person singular in its literal sense, but in behalf of all subjectivities.

5. As one of my colleagues has said, even the name itself would rule out the possibility.

6. This is admittedly clumsy language, but how else is one to say it? What verb is appropriate in describing how awareness takes up residence in men? Are awarenesses "had"? Are they "visited upon us"? Do they simply "emerge"? It is hard to say—literally. If only the adjective "aware" had its coordinate verb form, like "alive" or "awake"!

7. Alfred Stern, *Sartre, His Philosophy and Psychoanalysis* (New York: The Liberal Arts Press, 1953), p. 37.

8. Conte Giacomo Leopardi, *Song of the Wild Cock*, as quoted in Miguel de Unamuno, *The Tragic Sense of Life*, trans. by J. E.

Crawford Flitch (New York: Dover Publications, 1954; originally published in English in 1921), pp. 123–124.

9. The reader will be interested to learn that Sartre has devoted several pages in *Being and Nothingness* to a very serious ontological discussion of "holes."

10. Jean-Paul Sartre, *Being and Nothingness*, trans. by Hazel E. Barnes (New York: Philosophical Library, 1956), p. 22, author's italics.

11. *Ibid.*

12. Paul Tillich, *The Courage to Be* (New Haven: Yale University Press, 1952), p. 35.

13. Martin Heidegger, *Existence and Being* (London: Vision Press, Ltd., 1949), pp. 365–366.

14. Arland Ussher, *Journey Through Dread* (London: Darwen Finlayson, Ltd., 1955), p. 88.

15. Etienne de Sénancour, *Obermann*, as quoted in Unamuno, *op. cit.*, p. 263.

2

BASELESS CHOICE: THE
COST OF FREEDOM

The task is set: to live one's life, to assert one's selfhood, in such a way as to make nothingness—if that is what awaits us—an injustice. Now, just what would this injunction mean if it were translated into a practical program of living?

One can hardly begin this discussion without realizing that people exhibit differing attitudes toward the injunction itself, even before formulating responses to it. Let us grant, for example, that most people—maybe all of us—are devastated by the thought of being completely expunged from existence. Just or unjust, nothingness is so appalling as to be virtually unthinkable. This is to be taken literally: it is almost impossible to hold the thought of one's own annihilation in the mind for any length of time. And when, with effort, this thought is clamped in place and held before our consciousness, it can easily set off deep tremors in the spirit. Kierkegaard spoke of it as "fear and trembling"; Heidegger, as Dread; Sartre, as Nausea.[1] For want of better figures, these may be considered various names of a symptom, perhaps *the* symptom, of the anxiety or anguish we have just explored in Chapter 1.

But is this the only response we can make to the injunction? It is very easy to misunderstand Existentialism right at this point. Existentialism does not rest its case with trembling, with anxiety, or anguish, or all the other dreary metaphors—alienation, absurdity, homesickness—important as these notions are to the philosophy. It does not ask us, with the onset of the awareness of possible non-being, to lapse into a state of metaphysical blues. Rather, as a philosophy, it summons us onward, beyond these initial psychic states, to a new level of awareness: of self, of freedom, of choice, of responsibility, of authenticity. It summons us *to take charge of our own symptoms,* to assume personal control of our anxiety and make it the occasion for achieving a new kind of life.

It is this positive thrust of Existentialism which seems to have gone unnoticed in the beatnik atmosphere surrounding its reception in the United States. And we must retrieve the affirmative feature of the philosophy lest it be lost in the gobbledegook of trivial, "sweat shirt" advocacy on the one hand or self-righteous "Sunday supplement" scolding on the other. We must retrieve it if for no other reason than that here we may find the clues to an educational theory, which is what we eventually hope to fashion from this discussion.

THE QUEST FOR RECOGNITION

Each one of us, in the daily routine of business or in the larger tasks of life and career, wants recognition. We want to know that in some genuine sense we belong *to* and *in* the groups and activities with which we associate. This need is so powerful, as we all know, that if it is frustrated or unfulfilled for any length of time severe neurosis can result. Such understandings are now commonplace in psychological circles.

But what the psychologists seem to have overlooked, until just recently, is that this merely sociopsychic need is outranked in power and intensity by a need of an even higher order, what we might call a metapsychic need: Each one of us wants to know that in some genuine sense we belong *to* and *in* the *world*: we want to know that our existence is justified, that we are not *de trop*, not excess baggage, a useless surplus in the world; we want to know that our existence is not a chance event, not an accident, not an error of some kind.

Now, expressed in this fashion, the need for a sense of belonging-in-the-world may be thought of as a restatement of the paradox examined in Chapter 1. The need here portrayed is a kind of nostalgic yearning for some assurance that our individual existence has been taken note of, i.e., *recognized* as having occurred in the world. Ralph Harper has put it this way:

> *The heart of nostalgia is the belief in the irreplaceability of the individual—the real meaning of the hackneyed phrase, the dignity of man. But it remains true that every individual is replaced and is regarded by those closest to him as replaced, once he is out of the way. . . . It is inhuman to accept the total nonrecognition of death and personal loss, just as it is inhuman to believe and to act on the supposition that every man is replaceable. Man's dignity resides not only in his virtues, his freedom, and his justice but also in his belief that no one is completely replaceable. The aim of each individual should be to make this belief function in the world.*[2]

I think it would be possible to show that this craving for ultimate recognition, this need to believe in the irreplaceability of the individual, is the Prime Mover of all humanistic thought. Consider, for example, philosophy and religion. The bulk of traditional philosophy may be viewed as an attempt to explain the world in such a way as to convince man that he is in some way *necessary* to the entire scheme of things. His presence in the world is not only taken note of and thus recognized but given some ontological weight and warrant, so that human beings are portrayed as *required* in the world to render the whole of creation credible. In this sense, all philosophies from Plato to Hegel are what we may call "a priori humanisms." They not only presuppose the existence of man; they *insist* on it as a prerequisite to and essential feature of the cosmos. Going farther, if man is a rational animal, it must follow that he inhabits a rationalizable world; the existence of a reasonable being in a reasonless universe is a contradiction in terms. If this much be granted, then it can be conveniently turned around to assert that a rationalizable world without a rational being in it is equally preposterous. Hence, in one way or another, man must be considered ontologically necessary. In terms of "ultimate recognition," what more could man ask?

Well, it turns out that he *can* ask for more—and indeed he has done so! The complaint is that these philosophical justifications for our presence in the world are cold and impersonal. Classical philosophies are no more than elaborate cataloging systems in which everything somehow fits. The necessity for man's being is offered as a kind of logical or mathematical necessity. It is like saying that the system of Euclidean geometry, with its squares, triangles, and parallelograms, would not be complete without a trapezoid or that the numbering system from one to infinity requires a number seven to occupy the position between six and eight. But what comfort is that? What comfort is it to be told that one belongs in the world merely to round out the system, to fill a billet in some celestial table of organization? This clearly is not enough.

In the West, Christian theology has provided what was missing. It tells us that man needs recognition of a warm and personal sort. He wants not merely to be required in some "corporate structure" of creation but to be *wanted* and *cherished*, as a child is wanted and cherished by his parents. This is what the Christian God supplies, i.e., a supreme agent who not only recognizes our existence but is full of gladness at that very fact. He loves each one of us and his love does not have to have reasons, logical or mathematical; it is unconditional. Religion, then, supplies what philosophy by itself cannot offer, namely, transcendental love. And we find in this love the recognition and justification of our existence which we so desperately crave.

In our latter day, however, this, too, has failed to allay all anxiety. We have come to realize that the recognition so generously
distributed by a supernatural deity is really man-made. We discover that we have simply anthropomorphized a God into a God-
man-father and have equipped this ultimate being with the quali-
ties we very much want him to have, most importantly the ability
to love us without conditions. As Harper has remarked, "Christianity has . . . given man an excuse to hold himself dear."[3]

Thus, philosophy and religion have both miscarried. In an empirical and secular age, metaphysical necessities and anthropomor-
phic deities seem unconvincing. But the important thing to note
is that man still feels the need for existential recognition. So what
does he do? More sophisticated about destiny and possibly more
hard-boiled and on guard against fairy tales, modern man has decided to settle for something less. He has shut down his quest for
metaphysical or theological recognition and has chosen to seek recognition closer to home, i.e., here in the world of men. Culture
and society now represent the potential source of justification he
wants his existence to have.

*From the existentialist point of view, the present century is a
homeless century, in which men have lost the old points of recognition and seek, consciously or neurotically, new kinds of recognition. The several forms of totalitarianism of our time are intended
to be ways out of this spiritual homelessness for many millions. The
middle-class conventionality . . . is another way.*[4]

The term "middle-class conventionality" may be a trifle too pat
these days; American mores are plotted along coordinates not always related to class. But the general thesis is correct. We in the
United States find our identities almost exclusively in what we may
designate as *social* categories, in the affiliations we have entered into
with other individuals and groups in society. We are unquestionably, as David Riesman puts it, an other-directed, group-oriented,
organization-structured culture.

Consider for a moment the conversation you might strike up
with a stranger. What is the first thing you want to know? His
name. But then, when that is in, what next? Tell me, Mr. X, where
are you from? Where do you live? What do you do for a living?

Where do you work? Where did you go to school? Oh, do you know ———? The aim of these questions is to get a plot on the individual's social associations, to fix him against some sociointellectual background on the theory that to know him is to know his connections and his relations to other people. And then we respond in kind, proceeding on the same thesis. "Uh, yes. I'm from New Jersey. I'm on the staff at Rutgers University. I teach the history and philosophy of education." When I am done with this thumbnail autobiography, I am locatable in the scenery; I can be made out against the clutter and facelessness of a mass society.

But the cruel irony is that nothing important is really known about me. Only my affiliations are understood. These, my affiliations, are recognized, but *I* am not.

So we see that man's latest project, the attempt to find existential recognition among his fellows, has come to the same luckless end as his philosophies and his religions. Only this time there is a special pathos in his defeat not encountered in earlier trials, something that may help to explain why "age of anxiety," as an epithet for our time, has become so common as to be a cliché. The pathos is this: In settling for something less, in lowering our price for recognition and looking for it in human relations and organizational affiliations, we have been seduced into a kind of recognition which eventually takes away as much as it offers. For it is precisely in modern, corporate human relations and the impersonal organization complex that we become convinced, as we never were before, that we *are* indeed replaceable. Factory hand or college professor, store clerk or school teacher, it is the same; the organization *can* and *will* continue without you. And since "the organization" is somehow made to appear of higher rank than the persons in it, modern man knows he has been "out-psyched" by a counterfeit promise.

At this nadir, Existential philosophy has something important to say: These attempts to be recognized in the world—in philosophy, in religion, in society—were bound to fail! Why? Because they are all built on a faulty ontology of value.[5] This perhaps needs explaining. What it means is this: The craving for recognition (which we have examined in the last few pages) represents a desire that the *worth* as well as the *fact* of our existence be somehow acknowledged. To put it in first-person terms, I am absolutely certain of the fact of my existence; what I want to exact from an apparently indifferent universe is the further knowledge that my mere presence in the world is a good thing, that this presence shall eventually be recognized as having "made a difference" in the world. I realize, however, that my mere presence cannot, of itself, justify such knowledge. No, if I want to know that my existence "makes a difference," I must live my life in behalf of certain values; then, I believe, I will be *eligible* for the recognition I seek.

Now, when it is said that philosophy, religion, and social ethics are all constructed on a faulty ontology of value, we mean that they all have an erroneous notion of where the values by which I intend to live are to be found. These programs all start from the hypothesis that man is a *consequence of* the world rather than an *antecedent to* it. Believing this, they hold quite logically that man, qua consequent, must find his values in that of which he is a consequent, i.e., the world. They all begin looking for human values in the world instead of in men.

Classical philosophy looks for them in a set of independent categories that would go on existing even if there were no men. Religion looks for them in a superhuman being who personally underwrites the survival of certain values no matter how morally negligent men become.[6] Finally, contemporary social ethics looks for human values in institutional arrangements and in the social conventions necessary for effective group effort; the values according to which we are expected to live are those of the social system.

In every case, man's obligation is to something outside himself. Values are looked upon as entities already present in the ontic situation, entities to which he owes assent and allegiance. It is true that in social ethical theory man may be considered a participant in value making, but he is never considered in any of these three programs—even in the sphere of social ethics—*personally responsible* for the values on which he bases and orders his life. It is the inability to feel personal responsibility for one's own values that accounts for the bankruptcy of these three programs in granting recognition of the worth of our existence. The recognition they offer is eventually discovered by each one of us to be the recognition of something or somebody else—an ethical absolute, a God, or a social system. We, we find, cannot take credit for it. So we remain ineligible.

THE METAPHOR OF THE MORAL ADVISER

The Existentialist argument that the locus of value has been misplaced may possibly be made clearer by an analogy. When I seek recognition for the worth of my existence in the world, what I am actually doing is seeking advice on how to live my life so as to be eligible for this recognition. Seeking advice is the practical program I undertake as a means to the end of what I hope will be recognition. How does one go about seeking advice? I go about it in an existential setting in quite the same way I go about it in my daily routine: I ask somebody what to do. In general terms, I ask somebody, some "moral counselor," how I should live my life.

As we have seen, some people seek such advice in philosophic principles. Others seek it more directly in a God. Still others seek it in a social system. But the subtle deception of all of these efforts is that, whichever path one takes to get advice on how to live his life, he has already made up his mind what advice he wants by the mere act of choosing his adviser.

Consider, for instance, the situation of the President of the United States. In selecting his cabinet, he wants to gather about him advisers on how he should run the country. President Johnson did not have to select Dean Rusk as his Secretary of State; he could have chosen Richard Nixon or even Barry Goldwater. Why did he pick Rusk? The answer is simple. He did not want the kind of advice that he might get from Nixon or Goldwater. He wanted the kind of advice that Dean Rusk would be likely to give. In such a selection, therefore, the President stipulates in advance the kinds of policies he will follow in running the country, even before Secretary Rusk writes his first memorandum.

So it is with our personal lives. We seek advice and advisers. But if an individual goes to a priest, he has obviously already made up his mind what general outlines he thinks his moral life should take; he knows what kind of advice the priest will give. If another individual seeks out social convention as a guide to his conduct, he has already chosen the kind of moral life he wants to lead. In the mere *selecting* of the adviser, therefore, we in effect reveal to ourselves what advice we want for the shaping of our conduct. The final persuader to this argument lies in the prosaic but unexamined fact that, no matter how objective and impersonal our selection of an adviser is claimed to be, we still must decide, after the advice is given, whether to follow it or not! We are, therefore, eventually driven back to the starting point of all value decisions, namely, ourselves. And this is the inescapable conclusion: *I make my own advice.* The burden of Existentialism as a philosophy is to bring home to each individual the truth of this proposition.

VALUES WITHOUT BASE

To return to the basic problem of the search for values by which a life can be lived, it is clear that this search must be undertaken not in the outside world of "moral advisers"—philosophical, ecclesiastical, or conventional—but rather in the phenomenon of my own choosing. I may discover in the choices I make—in the things I do, in the attitudes I hold, in the goals I set for myself—I may find in these seemingly prosaic phenomena the values I have been trying to identify. In this sense, my problem turns out to be deceptively simple. Whereas I have been instructed in the past to look for values outside my choices, I discover under the aegis of Existentialism that the whole problem lies much closer at hand, i.e., in the way I individually live my life. My values turn out to be nothing more nor less than my choices.

And the point of the argument is just this: that in living my life I simultaneously identify those values on behalf of which I am living it. In the act of existing, I choose every day what I am going to do, what I am going to say, what goals I am going to pursue. To choose is, by definition, to set one alternative ahead of another; to choose therefore is by definition an exercise in valuing, an exercise in favoring this over that. It is in the very act of choosing that I point to those values which I wish to have listed on my "eligibility application" for recognition. But the difficulty is that I never know whether this or that choice is the one I should have made because there are no "advisers"—other than those I myself *choose*—to justify my choices. I am ultimately the author of all my choices, and since I can turn to no certifying agency to finally justify me in my choices, I discover that my choices are without base. They cannot be justified. I am a baseless base of values.

I therefore find myself in an odd position: I am the starter of the value-making process, but as such I myself have no base to stand on that can tell me which values I should start making. In this role, then, I discover that I am the originator, the inventor, the *creator* of values. And the oddness of my position is that I cannot help it; I cannot escape being the creator of values, for I cannot escape choosing in the world. Even to choose not to choose is a choice. I am therefore "condemned," as it were, to the peculiar role of being a chooser and therefore a value creator in the world.

In Chapter 1, you will recall, we had occasion to note that man is the being by whom "existence" and "nothingness" come into the world. We have now advanced to a point in our argument where we can see the practical meaning of this assertion, namely, that man, as existential chooser, is the being by whom values come into the world. *In the act of choosing, man brings values into being.*

In this sense, then, we may say that man creates something out of nothing. Consider a man in a situation. Before he chooses a course of action, there are no values in that situation; there is merely a value-free set of circumstances, a region of "pure phenomena." Once he chooses, he brings something new into existence: a "way of responding" to that situation. It does not matter what advice he got antecedent to his responding. In the final act he was the one who either accepted or rejected the advice, he was the one who responded, and he therefore was the one who brought a value into being in that situation. The value was not there before; now it is. And he is responsible for its being there.

Many people, even sophisticated intellectuals, somehow find the idea that man is the creator of values too extreme to believe. But is it really so bizarre? We may find anticipations of it in certain forms of the philosophy of Pragmatism. Listen, for instance, to William James. In the chapter on religion in his *Pragmatism—A*

New Name for Some Old Ways of Thinking he says that theologians and philosophers like to think of themselves as supremely rational; they like to insist that there must be reasons for contending that this or that object really exists in the universe. Then he says,

> But if one talks of rationality—and of reasons for things, and insists that they can't just come in spots, what kind of reason can there ultimately be why anything should come at all? Talk of logic and necessity and categories and the absolute and the contents of the whole philosophical machine-shop as you will, the only real reason I can think of why anything should ever come is that some one wishes it to be here.[7]

What this means is that even ontologies, of which the philosophical community has a great number, are constructed out of the "wishes" that are "fathers to the thoughts" of professional philosophers. If someone wants an ultimate principle, e.g., Jesus' *love* or Schweitzer's *life* or Marx's *dialectical materialism*, "to be here," it shall be here. So it is with values. If someone wants to introduce a value into the world, all he has to do is to live according to that value, and presto, it is "here."

THE MEANING OF BASELESSNESS

It is perfectly easy to see, therefore, that the creation of values is a very simple business. Every human being can do it—indeed, *must* do it so long as he is awake and choosing. The hard part comes in accepting personal responsibility for the authorship of one's own values and, specifically, accepting the notion that they are without base but are instead *original* with one's own life. In discussions of Existentialism, this idea of the baselessness and arbitrariness of human values is almost always the one that arouses protest. It is therefore worth some extended comment.

The difficulty seems to lie with the troublesome ambiguity of the word "arbitrary." In popular talk, it usually stirs up pejorative connotations of willful caprice, random stabbings in the dark, or malevolent ultimatums from some megalomanic dictator. People forget, however, that the word also means "depending on choice or discretion" (Webster's *Third*) or lacking an "adequate determining principle" (Funk and Wagnall's *New Standard*). Ignoring this area of the word's meaning, many Positivists and Experimentalists argue that arbitrariness does not infect empirical or experimental ethical theories because in these theories there is a continuous interplay between judgments and their consequences in action, between moral acts and the effects to which they lead. R. M. Hare, in his book *The Language of Morals*, explains this position by asking us to suppose, for the sake of argument, that a man, by some clairvoyance, can know all the effects of his acts beforehand.

> . . . *suppose that we were to ask such a man, "Why did you choose this set of effects rather than that? Which of the many effects were they that led you to decide the way you did?" His answer to this question might be of two kinds. He might say "I can't give any reasons; I just felt like deciding that way; another time, faced with the same choice, I might decide differently." On the other hand, he might say "It was this and this that made me decide; I was deliberately avoiding such and such effects, and seeking such and such." If he gave the first of these two answers, we might in a certain sense of that word call his decision arbitrary . . . but if he gave the second, we should not.*[8]

This analysis seems strangely unconvincing. Why is the second answer not also arbitrary? Granted, one can say that the man's *actions* are not arbitrary because they were done in the name of such and such effects. But how about the effects? Just how is one going to give reasons for his selecting certain effects as more worthwhile to seek than others? To be seeking such and such effects is to have already made selections from the total possible effects and to have established them as goals. It seems clear that the choice of desired effects is arbitrary and without justification, i.e., lacking an adequate determining principle.

Of course, it can be argued that such effects are sought in the name of still other effects, and these in the name of still others, until we come eventually to a "whole way of life" upon which de-

cisions are based. For example, I can refrain from shoplifting because I seek the effects of social behavior based on "the principle
of private property," and I value this principle because it makes
possible the effects of social behavior based on "the American social
ethic of free enterprise and 'to each his own,' " and I value this
ethic because it supports and furthers the effects of social behavior
based on the very meaning of "Western civilization," i.e., my
"whole way of life." Now Professor Hare seems to think that if no
justification is forthcoming for choosing this way of life, the man
cannot be charged with arbitrariness:

> *To describe such ultimate decisions as arbitrary because ex hy-
> pothesi everything which could be used to justify them has already
> been included in the decision, would be like saying that a complete
> description of the universe was utterly unfounded, because no fur-
> ther fact could be called upon in corroboration of it. This is not
> how we use the words "arbitrary" and "unfounded."*[9]

At this point we might ask Professor Hare to speak for himself,
or, better, to consult a dictionary. On the contrary, this is the way
a great many of us *do*, in fact, use these words. If a man comes to
a point in his thinking where he cannot give reasons for his beliefs,
we say such beliefs are arbitrary. If we are willing to take the
trouble, as Professor Hare apparently is not, to resist the pejorative
attitude, we may say that the man's beliefs are therefore *unjustified*
and *unfounded*, that is, without justification or foundation. This
does not mean that I am not entitled to believe in Western civilization as the best of all civilizations; it means merely that I cannot
offer reasons for believing it. A great deal of harm is done in ethical theory by implying that "arbitrary," "unjustified," and "unfounded" are terms of derogation.

The term "arbitrary" could, after all, suggest the presence of an
arbitrator or arbiter in a dispute. An arbiter is one who, after all
the facts are in and all the interpretations given, must *decide*. Of
course, it may happen that the arbiter bases his decisions on certain
"higher" principles. But in that case, the higher principles must
themselves be *chosen* by the arbiter; they are not forced on him.
In this sense, then, even if the arbiter offers a higher principle as

justification for his decision, he will eventually be unable to offer still higher principles to justify his selection of principles. At some point the justifying principle is found to be absent, and the arbiter is finally driven back to his own baselessness.

If this line of argument is unacceptable, the only alternative is to say that there is an ultimate, final principle upon which all arbiters' decisions are based. But if this were literally the case, no arbiter could call himself a free agent; he would be controlled in his decisions by this "ultimate, final principle." In the end, therefore, there would be no need for arbiters. All we would have to do would be to let the impersonal "principle" function in the dispute.

The absurdity of such a course is patent. Arbiters are brought into disputes precisely because a basis for settling them is lacking. It is the arbiter's task to function in the *absence* of an ultimate principle, a condition one might speak of as ethical nothingness, a phenomenal situation in which the very absence or nonbeing of something gives the situation its quality and eventually requires an arbiter to be called in. And what comes in? It is the free self of a human being, a free subjectivity capable of choosing and deciding. And in the deciding the free self (incarnate in the arbiter) simultaneously creates the principles which underlie the decision; in the act of deciding, that is, the decider reveals to himself the principles upon which he decides as he does. In that instant a self is creating values.

This allegorical side trip into the signification of the word "arbitrary" may help us to see how we function individually in the moral world. Each of us may be considered his own "moral arbiter" in shaping the course of his life. Moral choices are ultimately baseless and arbitrary, for I am the original author of the principles upon which I base my choices, just as the arbiter is. There appears to be no easy escape from this overpowering responsibility, for if there *were* a basic principle which I had *not* chosen, it would have to be a principle somehow written into the world to which I owed automatic allegiance. In that event I could no longer call myself a free agent. I would be in the thrall of a principle outside of me, beyond my reach. If I somehow *had* to believe that Western civilization was the best of all extant civilizations, I could not call this a free choice on my part. Hence, I could not really choose; I would be obligated to shape my conduct in a certain way. I would not be free.

We can see, therefore, that the claim to arbitrariness of our values, far from being a wicked hedonism, is actually the ground for there being any values at all in the world. The value-making agent in the world is the free subjectivity of man. He encounters a world that has no previous values written into it, a world that cannot offer values but can nevertheless be a "host" to values somewhat as a blank piece of paper can be a "host" to words. Man is the baseless base of values. And, though the price may appear to be prohibitive, baselessness turns out to be a priceless bargain. If it were not for this condition—that is, if there *were* bases and justifications—there could be no values, since there could be no real choosing.

In a somewhat analogous way, we may say that man's lack of an essence, his lack of a basic definition or "whatness," is at once his agony and his glory. If essence preceded existence, if the definition of man had somehow stepped into the world prior to the arrival of man, the whole human career would be easy: We would know what was right and what was wrong, what was human and what was not; we would, in short, know how to live. All we'd have to do would be to act out our human essence. But here is just the problem. If man's essence were already given, then we wouldn't be free; we would merely be acting out the destiny of man, speaking lines on a vast super-Shakespearean stage which had been written in advance for our utterance.

This is why the lack of an essence, while painful, is so rewarding. It is the agony we suffer in exchange for our freedom. It is what we pay for the privilege of writing our own lines in the drama, of being our own playwrights. And the paradox is that, even in our agony, we do not wish ever to find the essence of man. If we did find it, the whole human enterprise would come to a close and be over. There would be nothing left to do. All questions, moral and otherwise, would have been answered. Hence, all choosing would become superfluous—indeed, impossible—in a world where no alternatives were open.[10] Man—the chooser, the value maker—would dissolve and disappear and become merely an odd, hairless anthropoid, balanced on his hind legs, living out a prescribed existence.

AUTHENTICITY: THE AWARENESS OF
ONE'S FREEDOM

One may well ask at this point why we may not all be called unwitting Existentialists. If we are all subject to the "human condition" of essencelessness, what is so remarkable about Existentialism as a philosophy if its message is merely to announce this fact to us?

The answer lies in a curious but exceedingly important wrinkle of semantic logic concerning the word "choice." It is this: Choosing implies awareness on the part of the chooser. One cannot, by definition, "choose unawares." Hence, by definition, it is impossible to be an "unwitting Existentialist."

Suppose an individual finds himself in a situation and pursues a course of action which we shall designate A. Then his friend comes along and inquires why he didn't choose another course of action, B. To which our man says, "Oh, I never thought of B." Now, was he choosing between A and B? Of course not. Indeed, he was unaware of choosing at all. He was even unaware of possibly doing nothing, a course we may now designate as C. In this situation, then, although various alternatives were theoretically present, they were not present in his imagination, and therefore no choosing actually took place.

It is thus with our social and moral life. We are individually confronted in every waking moment by phenomenal situations to each of which there are numberless responses we could give. But the responses must rise as possibilities in our imagination before they can play a role in genuine choosing. Moreover, no choice is possible unless the free subjectivity is aware of the act of choosing as such. This means, therefore, that the free subjectivity must be aware not only of alternatives but of the *act* of considering alternatives before one may say that choosing is actually taking place. So-called "blind choosing" is a contradiction in terms. Pinning the tail on the donkey while blindfolded is not "choosing" where to put it. Nor does sheer impulse qualify as choosing; blurting out the first thing that comes to one's mind is not choosing. Nor is any mindless stabbing in the dark really choosing. *Guessing is not choosing.* "Choice" means selecting from alternatives in a state of awareness.

The claim that awareness is a necessary condition for choosing is simple common sense. More than that, in the awareness of choosing lies the subjectivity's very freedom! Unless an individual is aware of his act of choosing, he is not a free individual. The obverse of this would be plain nonsense. How could one be free if he were not aware of alternatives—if he had, he thought, only one alternative? To have "only one alternative" is another contradiction in terms. If a putative "alternative" is the only course of action, it is not an alternative at all. And to live without alternatives is to live without freedom, which is why it is so pathetic to hear someone say, "I had to do what I did; I had no alternative." He is either telling a lie or, through an act of self-deception, forfeiting his freedom.

We may summarize, therefore, by saying that awareness, choosing, and freedom are interlocking notions. By definition, they must all be present in the same degree. And they all finally come together in *the awareness of one's own freedom* in the act of choosing.

As it turns out, it is awareness of one's own freedom which helps explain who can and who cannot claim to be an Existentialist. That is to say, what differentiates people, in an existential sense, is the degree to which they exhibit such awareness. And we may now designate this global awareness as authenticity. People differ not in their susceptibility to the "human condition"; alas, we are all equals in this susceptibility. They differ rather in the degree to which they respond to the condition authentically, i.e., are aware of their freedom, aware of their baselessness, aware of their unjustifiability, and hence aware of their personal responsibility for the way they are living their lives. Some people, obviously, are numb to this sense of freedom. They do not see themselves as free agents in the world. Instead they explain their conduct in terms of values not of their own making—their culture, their religion, the expectation of their wife's relatives. What they forget is that they *consent* to those values. And in consenting to them, they in fact adopt those values for their own lives. But they are existentially unconscious; they are not aware that they are in fact consenting to something; they are not aware that they are free not to consent.

It is imperative not to be misled into thinking that the opposite of consent is somehow more existential. This is most certainly not the case. Revolt, rebellion, apostasy are not in themselves the mark of the existential man. Even the man who consents to convention can be the existential man *if* he is *aware* of the act of consenting, and hence of the necessity that he take *personal responsibility* for living his life in a conventional way. Most of us, let us admit, are of the conventional sort. We pull our socks on every morning with the expectation of fitting into community folkways throughout the day. Now, there is nothing particularly reprehensible about this behavior. What *is* reprehensible is our numbness to the fact that that very expectation is itself a value which we insert into our lives. So long as we do so unknowingly, unwittingly, we are nonauthentic individuals; we are not aware of making that value commitment at sock-pulling time.

Multiply the foregoing by all the other moments in life when situations call for the awareness of our freedom to choose our own personal response. The point is not to find the most deviant or bizarre response and to call that the "free" response. The point is to be *aware* of all responses so that when an individual makes his own response, even if it be supremely conventional and prosaically *un*bizarre, he will know that he has *chosen* something rather than simply fallen into it by necessity. It is the "necessity" people who will kill the human race—those people who say that this or that behavior pattern is required by God, or state, or mother-in-law. The people who say, "I couldn't help it; I had no choice," are the nonauthentics; they do not know they are human.[11]

And who is the authentic? The individual whose example is perhaps beyond the reach of most of us: the individual who is free and who knows it, who knows that every deed and word is a choice and hence an act of value creation, and, finally and perhaps decisively, who knows that he is the author of his own life and must be held personally responsible for the values on behalf of which he has chosen to live it, and that these values can never be justified by referring to something or somebody outside himself.

It is this imperative for *answerability* which is the leitmotif of the Existential argument. But how can we understand it? To whom is the authentic man supposed to be responsible? The answer is deceptively simple, I think, for the sense in which the word "responsibility" is used by Existentialists is precisely that of common speech. When we say to someone that he will be "held responsible" for something, we mean that if anyone should ask, he must be ready to answer for what he has done. The question of who might ask is irrelevant; maybe no one will. But in case someone does, he is to be ready to speak in behalf of his own performance.

Buber has put it this way:

> The idea of responsibility is to be brought back from the province of specialized ethics, of an "ought" that swings free in the air, into that of lived life. Genuine responsibility exists only where there is real responding.
> Responding to what?
> . . . We respond to the moment, but at the same time we respond on its behalf, we answer for it. A newly-created concrete reality has been laid in our arms; we answer for it. A dog has looked at you, you answer for its glance, a child has clutched your hand, you answer for its touch, a host of men moves about you, you answer for their need.[12]

Gabriel Marcel has developed the argument in a somewhat different way. He reminds us of the difference between making an observation and offering testimony. In making an observation, one is quite matter-of-factly speaking about events and phenomena beyond his own skin in which he has only the spectator's interest. But testimony involves observation, and more:

> . . . my testimony bears on something independent from me and objectively real; it has therefore an essentially objective end. At the same time it commits my entire being as a person who is answerable for my assertions and for myself. . . . I was present at the time and place of an accident; I can witness that the victim crossed at an island and that the car did not slow down; my testimony will throw light on the event and will help to assess the responsibility involved. I am obliged to bear witness because I hold, as it were, a particle of light, and to keep it to myself would be equivalent to extinguishing it. Can I refuse to attend the trial because of the

*trouble and the waste of time or because the victim was a stranger
to me?—I would be guilty of betrayal, but against whom? Against
society? . . . against the victim? but betrayal presupposes a commitment and I have no commitment to this stranger whom I have
seen by chance. . . .*

*What concerns us is the relation in which the witness stands to
the world. . . .*[13]

I think the relation in which the witness stands to the world
may be a clue to the manner in which the free subjectivity assumes
personal responsibility for his values. The witness can refuse to tes-
tify; he can claim that he didn't see anything or that he has forgotten. The free subjectivity can refuse to feel responsibility for the
way he lives his life; he can claim that he can't help it, that he
has to live his life that way. In both cases there is a basic dishon-
esty, a lie. But it is not a lie against another, or against society. It
is a lie against himself. For the witness knows that he *did* see something and that he *does* remember it; and the free self knows that
he *can* help it, he *could* live his life differently. The pathos is not
that the subjectivity has told a lie but that through an "intramural"
lie he has wiped out his precious humanness, his freedom.

Awareness of freedom is thus the main project of every life which
hopes to be existential. And it must be recognized by now that this
awareness requires us to take on a burden not easily carried. It is
the burden of *care*. To trade numbness for awareness is to feel the
intensity of moral involvement. It is to feel *personally* about life,
to feel the meaning of *personal* answerability, to *personally* care
about the increase of good in the world.

American society seems to encourage just the opposite mood.
Our organization complex is the victory of the *impersonal* social
apparatus of the corporation over the individual self. When a colleague gets sick at Rutgers, a Committee on Social Welfare sends
him a bucket of flowers and a "get well" card on behalf of the
faculty. It's almost like pushing a button on a vending machine:
word reaches the committee, a telephone is lifted from its cradle,
an order is placed, a messenger runs it over to the hospital, an
orderly delivers it to the bedside. When acknowledgment is re-
ceived from the laid-up colleague and announced in faculty meeting, a soundless wave of relief surges over the group. The
impersonal apparatus of the organization has taken "care" of our

personal cares; and each of us, potentially capable of being made aware of that person's misadventure, is made numb again by the cold, brutal form of corporate "sympathy."

There is, I think, a developing moral numbness in American life, a growing state of unfeeling in which we lose the sense of personal responsibility for protecting the safety of fragile human values in the close-in, person-to-person human relations that make up the routine of daily life. Instead, "human relations" becomes an objective science and public relations becomes another industry.

A world governed by "human relations" in the abstract sense rather than in the I-and-Thou sense of Buber is a world in which detachment replaces attachment as the leading value. As John Ciardi explains it, the "Playboyniks" who frequent the Playboy Clubs and the "Beatniks" who linger in the coffeehouses actually share a common ideology. They scorn the world of the "square." A "square" is one "who commits affection. . . . Both Boynik and Beatnik . . . are out to play it cool, the first with elaborate accessories, the second without. For both, however, the essential religion is detachment."[14]

In our time, it is too easy to become detached from other men. We increasingly think that Blue Cross can take care of the accident cases, CORE and the NAACP can take care of the Negro's fight for equality, and the Social Security Administration can take care of the weak and dispossessed. It's all so easy. "Care" has been incorporated; it is now a separate branch of public affairs.

Finally, to crown all, Norman Cousins of *Saturday Review*, who is otherwise a fairly sensible man, has come forward with the proposal that there be established a Society for Individual Responsibility! The mind boggles at such a suggestion—an organization to get individuals to be responsible! I can think of no proposal more likely to arouse Existential nausea, both organic and metaphysic, in the authentic man.[15]

ABSOLUTE FREEDOM

"Awareness" may be a matter of *degree*. Our lives are so much governed by reflex and routine it is difficult to say that anyone is wholly aware of choosing during his every conscious moment. Moreover, in actual experience we encounter some people who seem to have more active sensibilities toward the world than do others; some individuals concern themselves with the world's troubles while others are less involved. On a purely empirical basis, then, awareness might be said to be distributed along a continuum. But in that case freedom itself, since it rides with awareness, must also be distributed along the same continuum. In a manner of speaking, it is. But to grant this point may obscure another feature of Existential freedom which we can ill afford to miss, namely, that *freedom creates its own degrees*. An illustration may be helpful.

After listening to a discussion of the Existentialist's notion of freedom, someone is sure to ask if I am free to jump over the Washington Monument. The ingenuousness of his question both disarms and frustrates the argument, for it reveals an artless density in the questioner, as if he were expecting Existentialism to announce that the law of gravity had been repealed and thought he could score a point by reminding everyone that it had not. Any reader who feels that this is all Existentialism has to offer is asked to lay this book aside; the remainder of it will mean nothing.

I am obviously *not* free to jump over the Washington Monument. But this limitation may be due to the fact that I am not strong enough or to the fact that I have set out to do so. But which is primary? Where does my lack of freedom originate? It originates and is brought into being by my free choice to make this jump a goal of my life.

> . . . the coefficient of adversity in things can not be an argument against our freedom, for it is by us—i.e., by the preliminary positing of an end—that this coefficient arises. A particular crag, which manifests a profound resistance if I wish to displace it, will be on the contrary a valuable aid if I want to climb upon it in order to look over the countryside. . . . Without picks and piolets, paths already worn, and a technique of climbing, the crag would be neither easy nor difficult to climb; the question would not be posited. . . . Thus although brute things [like the Washington Monument] can from the start limit our freedom of action, it is our freedom itself which must first constitute the framework, the technique, and the ends in relation to which they will manifest

themselves as limits. . . . it is therefore our freedom which con-
stitutes the limits which it will subsequently encounter.[16]

Or consider the youngster in school who is told by his guidance counselor that his difficulties with mathematics are going to make it impossible for him to become an engineer. Just why does his lack of mathematical ability limit his freedom? The answer is foolishly simple—because he has chosen to become an engineer. It is his free choice of life goal which suddenly converts mathematical weakness into a limit. Suppose his choice had been "newspaper reporter." Would weakness in mathematics be a limit? Obviously not. It is thus the free choice of the individual which turns circumstances into either aids or limits to his freedom.

But at base, freedom is absolute because it is existential. And this freedom is the freedom to set goals. It is absolute because there are no limits to the freedom to set goals for oneself; there are no goals that one cannot choose. The setting of the goals comes first. Only later is this or that feature of the phenomenal environment recognized as a limit to accomplishing this or that aim in life.

The setting of goals may therefore be viewed as the starting point of value creation, the point at which values first peep through the soil. What then, to return to our opening question, is the practical program of living implied by the Existentialist injunction? I think it can now be stated as the project of waking up to one's freedom, of struggling up from the slumber of numbness and nonauthenticity to recognize that one is the architect of one human life and, through that life, the creator of values in the world.

It is not too early to say that an educational program built on this notion is what we shall call Existential.

NOTES

1. The capitalizations are designed to release a connotation of greater magnitude than the face-value lower-case metaphors would suggest.

2. Ralph Harper, "Significance of Existence and Recognition for Education," in N. B. Henry, ed., *Modern Philosophies and Education*, 54th Yearbook of the National Society for the Study of Education, Part I (Chicago: Published by the Society, 1955), pp. 220–221.

3. Ralph Harper, *Existentialism—A Theory of Man* (Cambridge: Harvard University Press, 1948), p. 9.

4. Harper, "Significance of Existence and Recognition for Education," p. 225.

5. Some individuals might interpret this as a kind of subtle counsel "not to be discouraged," as if the Existentialist were slyly building up to his own spectacular "solution" on the next page. Well, let the reader be advised: Take only limited heart at this point. Explaining why opposing views are incorrect says nothing about the correctness of one's own.

6. William James once remarked that "A world with a God in it to say the last word, may indeed burn up or freeze, but we then think of him as still mindful of the old ideals and sure to bring them elsewhere to fruition; so that, where he is, tragedy is only provisional and partial, and shipwreck and dissolution not the absolutely final things. This need of an eternal moral order is one of the deepest needs of our breast." *Pragmatism* (New York: Longmans, Green and Company, 1907), pp. 106–107.

7. *Ibid.*, pp. 288–289, italics in original.

8. R. M. Hare, *The Language of Morals* (London: Oxford at the Clarendon Press, 1952), pp. 58–59.

9. *Ibid.*, p. 69.

10. It is this quality which makes the concept of heaven so unappealing. There all problems have been cleared up, all indeterminacies resolved, all doubts removed; only sweet and certain serenity prevails. No ethical questions come up because they have all been answered. Moral puzzlement has at last been put behind. It is a place without problems. This seems to me a veritable hell.

11. Sartre gets particularly worked up about these individuals, calling them people of "bad faith," or *les salauds*, which is usually translated "stinkers" but which actually is a good deal stronger, more like the plural equivalent of our "son of a bitch."

12. Martin Buber, *Between Man and Man*, trans. by R. G. Smith (Boston: Beacon Press, 1955; originally published in England, 1947), pp. 16–17.

13. Gabriel Marcel, *The Philosophy of Existentialism*, trans. by Manya Harari (New York: Citadel Press, 1961; originally published in 1956 by Philosophical Library), pp. 94–96.

14. John Ciardi, "Manner of Speaking: Reflections of a Square," *Saturday Review*, Vol. XLVI, No. 44 (November 2, 1963), p. 10.

15. Mr. Cousins may possibly have gotten the idea from reading the "Personals" in the back of his own magazine. One of the more unusual of the running ads in this bizarre section reads as follows: "ARE THERE REASONS why humanists should join the American Humanist Association? We need members who are reluctant to join organizations. Introductory literature. Dept. SR7, Humanist House, Yellow Springs, Ohio."

16. Jean-Paul Sartre, *Being and Nothingness*, trans. by Hazel E. Barnes (New York: Philosophical Library, 1956), p. 482, italics in original.

3

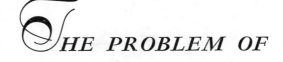

THE PROBLEM OF
"THE OTHER"

THE REEF OF SOLIPSISM

Any philosophy which builds its case on human subjectivity must expect to be challenged on one of the oldest of philosophy's problems, the charge of solipsism. As a philosophy, Existentialism is obviously vulnerable and it must navigate its way around this potential threat to its argument.

Just what is the difficulty? It may be explained in the following way. Whenever an account is given of the human condition, it is always a matter of arbitrary preference whether man's environing circumstances of nature and society or man's inner reflections on meaning and destiny are to be given the primary place. That is to ask, How do we best understand man? Do we understand him by peering outward, by first studying metaphysics or the natural sciences or anthropology, and then placing man in this or that context? Or do we understand him by peering inward, by studying his notions about himself as expressed in art or drama or literature, and then understanding the remainder of the world in his terms? In short, do we understand man in relation to the world or the world in relation to man? The history of philosophy must be conceived as a dialectic between these two programmatic approaches.

If we take the former path, we allegedly escape the charge of solipsism, for it is taken for granted that the world and other people genuinely exist; what is to be explained is how I, as a person, relate to that world and to those others. If we take the latter path, starting "from the inside and working outward," it is promptly recognized that each individual's perceptual understanding of the world will differ and that, in a manner of speaking, each person creates his own private world of meaning and destiny in which other people and objects play merely supporting roles. And, of course, since inward, subjective notions are never verifiable, they are true only for the individual who holds them. In principle, then, we are incapable of sharing each other's private worlds but must inhabit only our own. We are absolutely cut off from other individuals. To all intents and purposes, therefore, other people do not really exist in any objective sense; they exist only in one's private imagination. Hence the charge of solipsism.

Before proceeding to the Existentialist answer to the charge, it is important to notice that the traditional philosophies, for all their putative sophistication, have never really provided an acceptable answer to this problem. For example, realists and some idealists, preferring to understand the world first and then fit man into it, have merely practiced a benign self-deception by "taking for granted" the existence of the external world. With the assistance of this gratuitous assumption, they have talked themselves into thinking they are not open to the charge by the simple device of ignoring it. While this may be a good debating tactic, it is not a posture that serious philosophers can afford to strike.

Just how does the Existentialist deal with the problem of solipsism? A serious appraisal of the problem is likely to reveal a surprise: An acceptable way of thinking about solipsism is more nearly possible in the *second* of the above approaches, i.e., the Existentialist mode, even though on the face of things this approach seems to be, of the two, the less promising. Just how is this so?

In the opening chapter, it was asserted that "I am the first thing that is." This does not mean that I am the sole person that exists; rather, all other persons exist in my light. Our somewhat cryptic way of putting it may be better understood by referring to another of Sartre's vivid examples. Consider, he says, the phenomenon of shame.

> *I have just made an awkward or vulgar gesture. This gesture clings to me; I neither judge it nor blame it. I simply live it. . . . But now suddenly I raise my head. Somebody was there and has seen me. Suddenly I realize the vulgarity of my gesture, and I am ashamed.*[1]

It is clear from this example that my feeling of shame originates in the existence, either immediately or in my imagination, of other people. Shame is the seeing of oneself as seen by another; it is looking at myself in the same manner as I may look at another person.

Now note that the feeling of shame does not tell me about the existence of the other's merely *physical* presence; shame tells me of the presence of another *person*, another subjectivity. Ordinarily I do not feel shame in the presence of a dog or a cat because I do not attribute a free subjectivity to these creatures. Hence, I may indulge in all the vulgar gestures I wish with these animals without fear of shame.

And, of course, if one looks upon other people in the same way, as mere objects (as a master looks upon a slave or a tyrant upon a subject), then it is clear that he can avoid shame. But this is just the point—it is the very phenomenon of the subjective awareness of shame that tells us that other subjectivities are present in the world.

The same can be said for shame's counterequivalent, "fame." Suppose I win the plaudits of the crowd for a remarkable achievement, and my name is known and spoken in every province; I become famous. I feel intense pride in myself, I tingle at being a celebrity. This primary feeling can mean only one thing: There are other subjectivities like myself in the world who can look upon me as a famous person in somewhat the same way that I can look upon another as famous. My pride in myself, a favorable look at myself, is possible only in the presence of others. My pride is the phenomenal clue leading me to belief in the existence of other subjectivities. Before meeting his man Friday, Robinson Crusoe could not have felt either shame or pride except as he might have posited the existence of others in his world.

There is another, possibly more subtle, argument for the presence of other subjectivities in the world. It may be found in the existence of emotive language. If human language were exclusively cognitive in character, I would be able to look upon another human body as merely a duplicate of my own perceiving apparatus, an "experiencing machine," an answer-box. I would not have to assume the presence of a person or a subjectivity in the body I saw before me; he could be merely a highly developed biological cybernetic servomechanism. All of his cognitive behavior, including his so-called symbolic behavior of talking and writing and reading and listening, could theoretically be explained in terms of electrical relays.

But I am capable of evoking noncognitive behavior in that organism—I can make the body before me laugh or cry or snarl or blush. And what do these behaviors tell me? They tell me I have touched the region of *emotion* in that physical body, and I do it with emotive language, the language of communication between subjectivities.[2]

In sum, then, we may certify the presence of others—and I mean other *subjectivities*—in the world by the appearance in our experience of two phenomena: (1) private and personal feelings of shame or pride, which, by their very structure, require the existence of others, and (2) emotive language, which is capable of arousing and evoking feelings and emotional states in others. Thus is the charge of solipsism, if not refuted, at least neutralized. And the neutralizing has been accomplished within the frame of an introspective psychology, perhaps the least likely of places.

We come to a final polemic point: Just how do the realists, and the experimentalists too, for that matter, propose to answer the charge of solipsism? Demoting the role of the personal and private and introspective in their systems, they seem to be required to accept the existence of others merely on faith.

"HELL IS OTHER PEOPLE"

But now we catch an abrupt glimpse of an embarrassing irony: All this energy used to answer the charge of solipsism yields an unwanted victory, for it is the very presence of others in the world which qualifies and threatens my personal freedom. My status as a free subjectivity—what Sartre speaks of as "being-for-itself"—is put in jeopardy.

When I encounter the world, I encounter it as a subjectivity. My awareness of myself as an existing self in the world precedes all other awarenesses—a point that was established in Chapter 1. But this awareness means that the making of an essence for myself, my life's project, provides the additional awareness that I am a baseless chooser and value creator in the world—a point that was established in Chapter 2. Summed up, these awarenesses constitute my self as a *subject* in a world which appears to me to be made up of *objects*.

Among the objects I see are other organisms like myself in physical structure. But, as we have seen, my sense of pride or shame in their presence demonstrates to me that they exist not merely as objects but as subjects also. They are free subjects like my own subjectivity. Now, why do they threaten me?

They threaten me *as a subject* because with their look they turn me into an *object*, a *thing*. My vaunted subjectivity disappears and I become an object in their experience. I now recognize myself as playing a supporting role in *their* world, whereas before they had played such a role in mine. In this sense the other person, once he is seen by me as a subjectivity in his own right, is capable of turning me into a *thing*.

Allegorical evidence for this phenomenon abounds everywhere. We have already seen, in the cases of shame and pride, that we are suddenly turned into objects by the impact of the other's gaze, but the feeling is present in less spectacular circumstances. Consider riding in the subway. You are jogging along, staring into space in front of you or searching for something interesting to look at. You see faces across the car and just to amuse yourself you begin to study them. You make up stories as to what those persons are thinking, or what their plans are for the day, or where they are going. At the moment, you are complete *subject* beholding before you a set of objects. Then, by chance, you notice one of these people looking at *you*; he seems to be studying you in the same way you have been studying *him*. Your subjectivity collapses. You are sucked into *his* subjectivity. You are self-conscious, literally conscious of your self as being threatened by the other, who is conscious of you as an object. You wish he would look away.

Or consider the classic case of the keyhole. Suppose I am peering through a keyhole watching other people. They are, for me, at that instant mere objects, even more thoroughly objective than the people in the subway. And I am pure subject; I am beholding them, listening to what they say, interpreting their conduct, integrating the entire tableau into my subjective world of meanings. I am oblivious of myself as a being in the world. My attention is totally upon them as objective phenomena. Suddenly someone turns the corner of the hallway and sees me peering through the keyhole. At that instant the situation is abruptly and completely reversed. I become the raw object. My subjectivity is canceled; subjectivity arises in full force in the other who is looking at me. I am rendered a "thing." The only situation in which the collapse of my subjectivity could occur with more suddenness is that in which the door itself was opened, presenting me as the central figure in a small proscenium, caught in the awkward stoop of keyhole looker! Would it be possible to feel more like a thing?

It is understandable that human beings, with their creative ingenuity for novelty, should have invented extremely complex variations on the above phenomenon. Take, for example, one of the more poignant of our mass exercises in subject-object relations, the Easter parade on Fifth Avenue in New York City. Here is an interesting instance of what we may call "subjective self-deception." The individuals who go out upon the avenue on Easter Sunday do so ostensibly to see all the spring finery. Their real motive, however, is not so much to see as to be seen. They surrender at the outset their desire for subjectivity; they desire rather to become an object for that day, to be looked at and admired. But even this slender reward is withheld. Why? Because everybody else is doing the same thing. Everybody is being looked at, but nobody is looking!

Further documentation of the role of "the other" in our lives is unnecessary. The examples just given are enough to remind us that we individually experience the uneasiness of being "objectified" in varying degrees on almost any day. There is, however, a further dimension of the phenomenon which needs examining.

The awareness of "the other" does not so much delete my subjectivity as simply overpower it and bring into the front of my consciousness my awareness-of-myself-as-a-thing in another's world. And what I see with this awareness-of-myself-as-a-thing is the companion awareness that in that moment I lose my freedom. Whatever I do or say is done or said in relation to that other who still gazes at me and sees in my gestures or words the actions of an object in his experience. So long, therefore, as "the other" is present to me, my conduct must be interpreted as being carried on in his behalf. He therefore represents not only a threat to my subjectivity but a threat to my freedom. It is like being looked at through binoculars and seeing the binoculars looker as a speck far off in the distance. You would like him to turn away and watch something else, birds maybe—anything. But he continues to watch you. In this circumstance your every move is done *for* him; for the duration of his viewing you are an unfree thing in the world.

Because of the constant, potential threat that others represent Sartre has had one of his characters in the stage play *No Exit* remark that "Hell is other people." They represent the most inhuman of all possibilities: the assassination of my freedom.

Lest an overwhelming pessimism set in at this point, keep in mind that the threat to one's freedom is "possibility" only, not foregone conclusion. All I am trying to insist on here is the idea that, although man is, as we are often told, a "social animal," his "sociality" is not an unmixed blessing. I think it is better to live life with one's eyes open than to live it under an illusion, even if clear eyesight reveals a somewhat unhappy picture. Others *do* represent a threat to my freedom, and there is no sense in denying it just to make myself feel better.

The need now is to make clear the significance of this self-other relationship as it manifests itself at various stages on life's—and I mean *modern* life's—way. How is the threat to my freedom to be recognized in my various social relationships? I should like to examine this question as it applies first to man and society generally, then to man as a subject of the social sciences, then more specifically to man's personal relations, and finally to the intimate relations of man and woman.

MAN AND SOCIETY

By now it is a commonplace that we live in a mechanized, technologized civilization. It has been said, and repeated, and finally accepted that in such a civilization man must expect to become the appendage of his machinery. His responses in the most important area of his life, his economic behavior, must now be tuned to the impersonal, mechanical requirements of the production line. Man has always been a user of tools, but he has always understood that he directed the tool, and the tool was subordinate to his will. Obviously, in modern industrial manufacture this understanding has now been made irrelevant by the course of events.

It could be argued, perhaps, that the engineer is still the master of his tools, i.e., his machines. As their designer and builder, he stands to them in somewhat the same relation that the blacksmith once stood to his hammer or the artificer to his chisel. But the engineer differs from his earlier counterparts in that he is no longer the functional operator of the tools he designs and builds. And this is just the point. They are operated by other individuals who, because the engineer is sufficiently clever, do not need to know the rationale of the machine but merely its superficial behavior patterns.

These individuals, the workers, are the ones who have become functional appendages to their machines. Their behavior is dictated by the machine's rationale. In a manner of speaking, therefore, and without really intending to, the engineer has successfully turned other human beings into *things* through the esoteric rationale of an inanimate object. And this truth has not been lost on the twentieth-century laboring man. Perhaps even the modern history of organized labor can be instructive here. Would it be too preposterous to suppose that the violence and militancy of the organized laborer in seeking a measure of self-determination on such matters as wages and working conditions can be attributed, at least in part, to his discovery that self-determination in front of his machine was impossible? The engineer could inadvertently turn him into an economic object, but the plant manager could not, and the worker reacted accordingly.

The truth of all this is so patent as to hardly need saying. And the present sweep toward automation can only intensify the difficulty. The possibility of mass unemployment is bad enough, but even if all are kept working, their sense of being used in an automated productive process cannot help increasing.

Of somewhat more recent origin is the recognition—again so obvious as to need little comment—that we work and live in an "organization" society. But we must not misunderstand this: the organization way of life is a threat to a personal freedom not simply because the individual cannot control the organization's goals and purposes; it is a threat because of a more profound characteristic of organization as such, namely, the necessity to consider individual human beings replaceable. As pointed out in Chapter 1, the pathos of modern life is to be found in the fact that our request for recognition is answered by a cultural ethos of organization, and the central principle of this ethos is that social processes can be rationalized in somewhat the same way as productive processes, that is, through the rationalizing procedures of the so-called "social engineer." Organization, then, is not merely a group of individuals coming together to get something done. Rather, it is more profoundly *a theory of dealing with human beings*, a theory which embraces the technological principle of the interchangeability of parts and raises it to a high art. It is this quiet whisper of the organization mentality that men are interchangeable—and on fairly short notice—that finally eats into the spirit of the human person. If the whisper is repeated often enough, and of course it must be in organization life, sooner or later the individual will come to accept the fact that he has been turned into a *thing*.

If men can become things by virtue of being appendages to machines or functionaries in organizations, they can also suffer the same unhappy fate by the more subtle and informal process of overadjusting to the expectations of those about them. We call it, of course, conformity. Here again the humdrum repetition of this cliché tends to cloak the real difficulty. It is not conformity itself which threatens human freedom but rather the nature of our awareness concerning conformist behavior. To refer once again to Ralph Harper:

> . . . middle-class conventionality . . . does not depend on a systematized authority, but rather on the individual adjusting himself constantly to customs and even fads. There is no room for eccentricity in middle-class America, "unless one can afford it," any more than in a totalitarianism. And eccentricity, which in itself is not the noblest of virtues, is forced into a position of empty prominence by the fact that conventionality requires everything and gives nothing.[3]

". . . eccentricity, not the noblest of virtues. . . ." How profoundly understated! Is the eccentric more safe from the threat to his freedom by "the other" than is the conformist? Of course not. He may be indulging in eccentricities *for the sake of "the other"!* How many eccentrics there are who are merely exhibitionists! And eccentricity can even become its own institutionalized convention— in beatnik culture, for example. No. The point is missed in all this. Neither conventionality nor eccentricity makes me unfree; it is my *awareness* of "the other" which is crucial in this determination. Ask the question: Is the presence of "the other" seducing me into convention or eccentricity? If so, I have accepted an unfree relation toward him and become a *thing* in the world. But if I have authentically chosen a course of behavior which is my own, the result of a baseless choice on my part, and which turns out, after the fact, to be conventional or eccentric, obviously I have kept my freedom intact.

Conformity, then, must be understood as only the surface phenomenon of our age. Beneath it lies the threat of "the other" made known to me through my awareness of him. If I can hold "the other" at bay, so to speak—that is, if I can dismiss the awareness-

of-the-other from my mind temporarily while I make my choices—
it will not matter one way or the other whether the course of action
I choose turns out to be either conformist or deviant. It will still
be mine, freely chosen and therefore genuinely authentic in the
shaping of my life's project.

Put in plain language: If I freely choose to conform, if I enter
into and appropriate for my own life the conventions of my society, *and* if I take *personal responsibility* for them as values in the
world which I create by actually living them, then I can claim an
authentic life. It is when I weaken and yield to the gaze of "the
other" and simply follow the conventional path tramped down in
front of me that my freedom as a man is put in jeopardy. Likewise,
if I decide on some odd or irregular behavior merely because of the
effect it will have on other people's estimate of me, I am still of
"bad faith"; I have forfeited my free project and turned it into a
stage production for an audience. It is theirs, the others', not mine.

MAN AND THE SOCIAL SCIENCES

One might suspect from this analysis just what can now be said
about any science which claims to call itself "social." Such a science
must be, by definition, the climax to the process of turning human
beings into things.

Man began his science with the objective phenomena of his
world—with stars and rocks and trees and frogs. Later he turned
to more sophisticated "objects"—matter and motion and energy.
Always on the lookout for new worlds to conquer, he finally stum-
bled upon himself, and the discovery was like the finding of gold!
It set off, as we all know, a pell-mell, headlong "land rush" into
every cranny of human conduct, from perception to morals. As with
the invention of the printing press in the history of knowledge,
all hell broke loose! The social sciences have descended on us like
an avalanche, and within only the last seventy-five years.

Now that we have time to look back and assess this "Coperni-
can" moment in the history of science, we can see that the discovery was of man as an *objective fact* in the world, a behaving
organism whose behavior was, at least in principle, open to public

inspection in somewhat the same way as is the behavior of stars and frogs and molecules. Therefore, the so-called human and behavioral sciences of sociology, political science, anthropology, and psychology are, in strategy and method, the same as the natural sciences of astronomy, biology, chemistry, and physics. They study a different sphere of phenomena, to be sure, but they study such phenomena much as the natural scientist studies his, i.e., as objects in motion in the perceptual world.

It would be neither fair nor prudent to scorn the insights we have secured from the behavioral sciences and to write them off, the way some people do, as worthless. On the contrary, these understandings have made possible some startling and, by and large, beneficent forms of control in social affairs. The smoothing out, for example, of violent fluctuations in the economy, which the political economists appear to have mastered, certainly must be credited with preventing a great amount of human suffering, notwithstanding the fact that much economic misery still persists in our society.

The problem of man as an object of science lies somewhat deeper, and it relates not to this or that facet of human behavior which is brought under study but rather to the very nature of science as a mode of inquiry.

Science is inevitably reductionistic. The aim of science is to generalize, but every generalization is a simplification. Science does not deal with individual entities in their uniqueness; it deals with classes of beings distinguished and defined entirely in terms of shared properties. . . . The essence, if I may use this old-fashioned word, of the individual man or the individual social fact escapes classification.[4]

The necessity for science to stick to the "shared properties" of men signifies, or should signify, for every human scientist a sad and sobering truth: Science is inevitably limited to that which is relatively trivial in the human sphere. If science tells me that a certain proportion of the population will behave in a certain way given a certain set of circumstances, it tells me something that is unquestionably warranted (if the procedures are correct) but relatively unimportant.

I should say that the problem does not stop here. For science, at least the way it has been advertised in the last half-century, is organized toward the ultimate aim of "prediction and control." The shared properties of classes of men are plotted and cataloged with such precious patience not merely to find out interesting things about people but to suggest specific lines of social action. A candidate takes an opinion poll of his constituency to shape the content of his campaign speeches. A psychometrist examines a group of boys and girls with a standardized test to determine the learning experiences they should have. A manufacturer does market research on his clientele to decide what products to push. And, yes, a Federal Reserve Board economist studies the citizenry's economic habits to suggest to the President what policies to follow in controlling fluctuations in the business cycle. In every case, even when the action is taken in behalf of human welfare, the ultimate result is to show the constituent, the boy or girl, the customer, or the citizen that he is vulnerable to being treated as a thing, as a counter in a huge game of Monopoly.

Consider also the television program "Candid Camera," built on the principle that there is entertainment value in the behavior of people who are unaware of being observed. It is the "keyhole" principle carried to its logical limit by the mass media. What is left unsaid is the deeper truth that human beings presented to us in this fashion are reduced to the status of animals in a zoo. The fact that the American public does indeed find this phenomenon entertaining probably should not surprise anyone. But the fact that the individuals shown on the program have all signed releases for their appearance *should* surprise every one of us. At the very least, it tells us something about these individuals; it points to the possibility that their human subjectivities are in a weakened condition and that they do not mind being treated as objects for others' amusement.

One final illustration. A few years ago, there was a great public outcry at the publication of the Kinsey reports on sexual behavior in the human male and female. For all the insights these two reports provided us, the outcry may have been in part a protest against treating men and women as laboratory specimens. Kinsey certainly had a knack for removing all feeling and emotion from his prose. Especially in his work on the male, I found I had to keep reminding myself I was reading about real, live people instead of marmosets or rabbits. As it turned out, Kinsey acknowledged this aspect of his work, and when the publication of his second volume, on the female, was announced he assured the reporters present that it was "more human." To which some female commentator is alleged to have remarked: ". . . a little *too* human." She was, of course, entitled to her own opinion. But we may see a kind of truth in her jocular, double-entendre rejoinder, namely, that even if one is beyond all Puritan squeamishness there is a certain repugnance to the idea of converting orgasms into statistics.

In the social sciences "the other" is represented by the researcher. He is the Big Eye who gazes. He is honored in this country because he has adopted the established religion of science. And since science knows only one way of studying phenomena in the world, i.e., as objective and outside the emotions of men, the social science researcher has acquired undreamed-of power in threatening human freedom. He is capable, in one stroke, of turning vast groups of human beings into statistics, into mere numbers on a sheet of graph paper. He can announce, "I'm going to make a survey!"

MAN AND FRIEND

We come now to what we might call "close-quarter" human relations, the fragile ground on which person encounters person. At the outset, I suppose there would occur to the reader some incongruity in attempting such a discussion under the aegis of the Sartrean principle that "Hell is other people." Can friendship be understood, it might be asked, under the illumination of such a seemingly belligerent attitude? I think the answer must be "Yes"; and the surprise will be that, in the next section, we may even understand love itself more completely by approaching it from what many might think to be its darkest side.

First of all, we must be sure to straighten out our lines of communication. When Sartre speaks of hell as being other people, he means, as we have seen, that other subjectivities are theoretically capable of objectifying me and turning me into a mere thing in their experience. But this does not mean that another subjectivity[5] *always* does this to me. It does not rule out the possibility that another subjectivity could actually encounter me as a subject! Indeed, this is precisely the possibility that we now wish to explore, and I have already hinted at it in commenting earlier on the existence of emotive language, the communication device by which subjectivities make contact with one another.

Also, by way of foreword, we may call to mind Martin Buber's equivalent analysis. Man, he says, has two "primary words": (1) I-Thou, and (2) I-it. These "primary words do not signify things, but they intimate relations."[6] They "do not describe something that might exist independently of them, but being spoken, they bring about [the] existence" of these relations. The first of the primary words, I-Thou, refers to the relation between subjectivities; the second, I-it, refers to the relation between a subjectivity and an object. And, of course, it is the former relation to which Buber has devoted an entire work (*I and Thou*) and indeed an entire career. Perhaps no phrase epitomizes his thought better than the oft-quoted "All real living is meeting."[7] Not the mere saying of "Hello," but the intimate encounter of person with person, subject with subject.

A third preliminary reference should be made—to Gabriel Marcel. His counterposed notions are *object* and *presence*. We all understand, he says, what it means when I say that something is an object in my experience; and, of course, other people may occupy this category, say, on a crowded street or sometimes in the same room. But we also know what it means to say that a person's "presence is felt." It means that the person sitting beside me or the person a thousand miles away is somehow present in my psychic experience. He is there not as a sentient body among other bodies but as a center of feeling and sensibility, another subjective "pole" of awareness to which I refer as a subjectivity.

Marcel, after discussing "charm" as a special instance of presence, puts it this way:

> . . . when we say that a presence must not be thought of as an *object,* we mean that the very act by which we incline ourselves towards a presence is essentially different from that through which we grasp at an object. . . .[8]

He uses the words "incline" and "grasp" advisedly: Concerning an object, I can grasp it or not; I can literally take it or leave it. But a presence is something "leaned toward," something felt, an awareness not taken or left but somehow experienced in the inner regions of my subjectivity.

We see, therefore, that there is no incongruity among Sartre, Buber, and Marcel. They are all talking about the same dimension of intersubjective experience. And they all recognize that "the other" can understand me in either of these two ways: as a subject, a "being-for-itself," or an object, a "being-in-itself" (Sartre); a "thou" or an "it" (Buber); a "presence" or an "object" (Marcel). "The other" represents a threat when he sees me as an "in-itself," an "it," an "object." He represents the diametric opposite of a threat, i.e., the very medium of my subjective becoming, when he sees me as a "for-itself," a "thou," a "presence."

Having established these understandings, what can we now say about "close-quarter," person-to-person relations? It is obvious that the bulk of our experience with other people is in the "I-it," "subject-object" mode. That is to say, other people move through my region of experience—at work, in the community, in public places—more as organic objects than as human selves. Especially at work, other people stand for functions to be performed, and they relate to me in that way. And, of course, I to them in the same manner. (As I write this, my secretary is seriously ill and on leave from her position in my office. My relationship to her has been sharply altered; whereas before she was an effective and intelligent colleague performing a vital function in my particular corner of institutional life, she is now a person, a self no longer to be understood in terms of the tasks she performs but rather in terms of the feelings she feels, the attitudes she exhibits, the moods of despair or optimism she makes known to me through her "presence" over the telephone. And she now has a new relationship to me; instead of a superior from whom she has standard expectations of behavior, i.e., instructions to follow, work to perform, letters to write, I am now another person in her sphere of personal acquaintances and interested in her welfare. Her apologies about falling ill and her "being sorry for leaving you in the lurch at such a busy time of year" all seem somehow utterly irrelevant to our new relationship.

Standing formerly to each other as functionaries, we have temporarily suspended this relation in favor of a "subject vis-à-vis subject" relation.)

One of the more poignant instances of this phenomenon of standing to others as a function instead of a person may be found in the classroom itself. The college professor, oblivious of the impression he makes, does not realize that the college student sees him as a "talking machine," a kind of "knowledge-dispensing apparatus" whose headaches, anxieties, and general animus have been so successfully filtered out of his lectures as to give credence to the notion that he must be a creature incapable of love or heartbreak. Consider the professor's alarm, then, when, under more informal social circumstances, students seem to "discover" the presence of feeling in him almost unexpectedly—as if the professor's subjectivity were something of a surprise—and they blurt out: "Why, you're really human!" There is no professor anywhere for whom it would not be troubling to learn that there has been some doubt about it.

Once we fight loose from function and stand clear of it, it then becomes possible to enter into a "subject vis-à-vis subject" relation, a relation which is, as we all know, one of the more fragile in human affairs. If it is made permanent, it becomes the relation to which we give the name "friendship." A friend is another subjectivity whom it would be impossible to treat as a thing or set of functions. If "blood is thicker than water," as they say, then certainly "water is thicker than (what shall we say?) air." That is, my obligations to my kin come first; but after that, my obligations to a friend outrank and have priority over any obligations I might have to the impersonal society around me. I cannot report a friend to the police no matter what he may have done. And to understand this is to understand why Dean Acheson, Secretary of State under President Truman, could say, concerning a convicted spy of the 1950s, "I will not turn my back on Alger Hiss." It would be a contradiction in terms to speak of "turning one's back" on a friend.

The fact that the American people found Acheson's remark so difficult to comprehend may tell us something about the precariousness of really deep friendship in the modern world. Is our time and place, one might ask, witnessing the slow evaporation of this quality in intersubjective experience? Or, put another way, is social evolution developing in such a way in America that the opportunities and chances for really close friendships are gradually being legislated out of existence? To look around, it would seem so. And the social commentators appear to be confirming our private impressions; they are speaking of the difficulty of permanent interpersonal relationships in a society as mobile, mechanized, and depersonalized as ours. Could it be that we live such an efficient, smoothly functioning, socially engineered existence that we can't *afford* deep involvement with others?

In this connection, I once remarked to the students in one of my university classes that the contemporary world offers an ambiguous mixture of blessings. We are steadily thrown into contact with more and more people, yet the number of acquaintances with whom we could find it possible to become close friends seems to be decreasing. I believe this to be true myself, but I was startled by the nodding heads and the assenting glances. There is a certain sadness in learning that twenty-year-olds, just starting out on adult life, have already discovered, rather before their time, a troubling truth about their world.

MAN AND WOMAN

But if this is the precarious character of friendship in the world today, man still has available to him the most intimate of all subject-subject relations, namely, love. I suppose this is the "test case" of the Existentialist's analysis of the role of "the other" in human experience.

It is necessary that we make some very plain and straightforward observations about male and female concerning their relations to each other as subjects or objects. To start with, it is obvious that the female is more susceptible to being turned into a thing. At least in the Western world, especially in America, she is expected to be *looked at* in the most literal sense of this phrase. Not only that; she is taught that being looked at is one of the highest values in her development as a female. To be the object of another's gaze, to be watched and admired and coveted—these are the ends toward which a great proportion of female behavior is directed. And, as we all know, they have been capitalized upon by American cosmetic ingenuity, so that today a vast industry has sprung up to answer this urgent female need.

It is illuminating to consider for a moment so prosaic a subject as clothes. In a Sartrean analysis, covering our bodies with clothing is the not so subtle way we have of shielding our object-ivity from others. "To dress oneself means to dissimulate our object-character, to claim the right to see without being seen, the right to be a mere subject."[9] The curious irony consists in the fact that the female employs clothing for precisely the opposite effect, to enhance and attract the gaze of others, to turn herself more completely into the object of another's observation.

Of course, all this could be attributed to social conditioning, and it would be difficult to deny that culture has a lot to do with it. But there may be more to it than that. Is there something in woman's very nature, perhaps interlocked with her natural function of childbearing, that necessitates her assuming the role of a "natural object" in the world? Many women seem altogether too anxious to look at themselves in this light, as if they were some kind of necessary cog in a fixed natural order, and their chances for self-determination were somehow radically foreshortened or withdrawn with the accident of their having been born female.

Professor William Barrett has a strange way of agreeing with them:

> *What sense does it make to say that . . . a woman's identity is constituted by her project? Her project is family and children, and these do in fact make up a total human commitment; but it is hardly a project that has issued out of the conscious ego. Her whole life, with whatever freedom it reveals, is rather the unfolding of nature through her.*[10]

Barrett goes on to agree with Sartre that man exists by extricating himself *from* nature, but since the same assertion cannot really be made about women, Sartre's psychology "shows itself indeed to be exclusively a masculine affair."

But Barrett, and the women he is agreeing with, forget something. To get free of "the unfolding of nature" through one's own body should not be all that difficult; certainly it cannot, or at least *need not*, take up the "whole life" of the modern woman. This "whole-life-at-the-service-of-nature" theory is what Betty Friedan calls "the feminine mystique." And she argues against it with persuasive, if perhaps overstated, rhetoric in her book of that title.[11] The point that Barrett should have made and that Friedan does make is that if woman is totally implicated in nature, that is, plugged in via an unseverable extension cord to the natural world, it must be because she has consented to, i.e., actively *chosen*, that relationship.

A great deal has been written in the twentieth century on the modern woman, her problems and her future. She is periodically the subject of television documentaries, learned conferences, serious magazine articles, and erudite books. But these accounts all fail to reach the heart of the difficulty.[12] The problem of modern woman has its origin in her susceptibility, no doubt fomented and stupidly encouraged by men, to the idea that she may legitimately consider herself an object instead of a subject in the world.

But this is a picture of woman in her more or less public moments. The more private moments of male and female, in love and marriage, offer a more likely place to make the final test of the Existentialist analysis of the subject-subject relationship.

Let us put the matter bluntly: Marriage is a contract of *possession*. We want to possess the other party. We want to possess him or her in the sense that we want that person permanently *present* in our lives. This desire should be taken literally. We want to know that "in sickness and in health," when we speak the name, another subjectivity will respond by saying, "Present. I am here."

Yet, there is an ambivalence to this desire. Although we want to be sure of, to depend on, the person's presence in our lives, we want that presence to be the *free project* of the other subjectivity; we want the other subjectivity to freely choose to be present. But if being present is a free project, that presence can always be withdrawn; it is contingent and not certain. So marriage becomes a strange game of phantoms: "The lover does not want to possess the beloved as one possesses an object. He wants to possess her as a subject, a living freedom."[13] And here is precisely the difficulty: "Love wants to possess the other self's freedom *as* a freedom."[14]

How, and under what logic, could such a remark possibly have any meaning? To possess a freedom is a contradiction in terms. It is like "possessing" a handful of mercury.

To possess an object, in male-female relations, is common enough, as is obvious in the house of prostitution. But a man of only average sensibilities can find no real enjoyment in a prostitute. He can possess her only as a thing-with-functions. Her presence is an unfree relation; it has been purchased. She is an entertainment gadget, not a person. Prostitution is an evil, therefore, not because it is sexual but because it succeeds as few other occupations do in turning human beings into things.

But to possess a subject—this is the goal of genuine love. And yet, it is an impossible goal! Freedom cannot be possessed.

At this point Existentialism rests its case. Why? Because nothing rational can be said beyond this point. Reason is no longer relevant. For, even though love is impossible, it exists in the world! It is the wizardry of subjectivity in the world to be capable of possessing other subjectivity. Subjects do *possess* and *belong to* other subjects. And reason cannot account for it. Reason is neither adequate nor inadequate. It is totally irrelevant.

We have a right to believe, therefore, that human love is the most remarkable phenomenon in the world. Not exactly empirical, yet somehow present in our experience, love is that wordless language of subjectivities, that transrational, but very real, phenomenon of subject making ultimate contact with subject.

MAN AND GOD

By way of an unscheduled postscript to the foregoing, we may conclude by indicating the manner in which "the other" appears to man in its ultimate, universal form. In so doing, we may catch a glimpse of the often-inquired-about difference between a theistic and an atheistic Existentialist.

At the outset of Chapter 2 we examined the need for recognition as it expresses itself in human subjectivity. This need, historically, has evoked a number of "answers," one of them primarily religious. Indeed, organized religion's very essence, its *apologia pro vita*, is its alleged capacity to make believable man's hypothetical hunch that he is somehow irreplaceable in the universe. The important thing to note about religious, in contrast to philosophical or social, forms of recognition, however, is that the recognition emanates from a subjectivity rather than from an impersonal idea or a collective ethic. Hence, the Christian God had to be a *Person*, which we may now designate as a supernatural "Other," to whom all men may relate as subjects.

Now, the theistic Existentialist is inclined to feel that God-as-Person, God-as-Subjectivity, God-as-Ultimate-Other must be understood not as a truth but as a kind of "hypothesis of the spirit." We are unable to feel the presence of the subjectivity of God in the same literal sense as we can feel the presence of other human subjectivities. We must settle for something less: the *possibility* of that presence in the world. We are caught, as it were, between desire and logic. We are left only with hope. We must live our lives *as if* the Ultimate Other were present, *as if* the world contained the quality of subjectivity which would be needed in the event that ultimate recognition, rather than nothingness, were to be granted. A life lived under the "as if" is admittedly precarious. But man is entitled to at least this much, little as it is, if for no other reason than that without the "as if" the human search for meaning would itself be a form of insanity. The important thing, says Paul Tillich, is to have "ultimate concern for the ultimate." Wherever that concern is manifest, there also will one find the ground for a possibly authentic life.

The atheistic position is somewhat more straightforward and takes a rather surprising form: The question of God's existence is beside the point!

> *Existentialism isn't so atheistic that it wears itself out showing that God doesn't exist. Rather it declares that even if God did exist, that would change nothing. . . . Not that we believe that God exists, but we think that the problem of His existence is not the issue.*[15]

Man still has to choose, no matter what Gods are present. Moreover, he has to choose his Gods! Even the "as if" is bootless. Man still must make his own project. It makes no difference, therefore, how one thinks about God's existence; the issue lies elsewhere, in how one is to live one's life.

There is one possible difference God's existence could make, says the atheist, and it is wholly unacceptable. God's presence in the world is an attractive notion only so long as he encounters me as a being-for-itself, a "thou" to his "I," a free subjectivity. But that would be impossible. If he made me, i.e., if he is responsible for my being, he could view me only as an "it," as another object in the world. His gaze, therefore, since it is all-seeing, threatens me totally. His look destroys me as a freedom and turns me into a thing. If "no sparrow falls but God knows of it," then I, like the sparrow, am constantly in the sights of his binoculars. I am permanently trapped, converted absolutely into a thing.

Billy Graham explains himself to his audiences by saying that he is "the instrument of God's purposes," that "God's will is working through me." There is a certain chill and pathos to these utterances. According to this view, God *uses* men; he manipulates them as instruments. If such be the case, then it is contradictory for any man to consider himself a free being.

NOTES

1. Jean-Paul Sartre, *Being and Nothingness,* trans. by Hazel E. Barnes (New York: Philosophical Library, 1956), p. 221.

2. The popularity of jokes about electronic computers and data processors may be indirectly instructive. These jokes usually concern the surprising presence of a subjective element in these devices: e.g., (1) *New Yorker* cartoon showing shaken scientists reading the first "ticker tape" from their brand-new electronic brain which they have just installed and turned on; the tape says, "Cogito, ergo sum." (2) IBM, RCA, and General Electric decide to wire the circuits of their largest computers in series and to put some really tough questions to the elaborate combination. The first question they feed into the machine is "Is there a God?" After much whirring and humming and blinking of lights, out comes the answer: "There is *now!*"

  If the day comes when such answers really do come from the machines, alarums will be in order; even so, we will still have a little time left. But let some engineer's programmed input result in his monster's responding with a belly laugh or a tearful "Boo-hoo" punched in code on the tape—*that* will be the day to consider surrender.

3. Ralph Harper, "Significance of Existence and Recognition for Education," in N. B. Henry, ed., *Modern Philosophies and Education*, 54th Yearbook of the National Society for the Study of Education (Chicago: Published by the Society, 1955), p. 226.

4. Robert G. Olson, "Science and Existentialism," an address delivered to the student body of Douglass College, Rutgers University, on October 17, 1963.

5. I am all too aware of the fact that by using the word "subjectivity" in its substantive form I seem to be reifying it and giving credence to the erroneous notion that it stands for some specific definable element in the world. That is, I am in danger of making an object out of subjectivity. I know no way to avoid this, given a language such as English in which nouns, which we are virtually required to use, carry so much freight of Aristotelian essence with them. If we can understand the phrase "another subjectivity" to stand for a phenomenon in the world whose presence I can feel but whose definition is inscrutable, I think we can get on with our discussion.

6. Martin Buber, *I and Thou*, 2nd ed., trans. by R. G. Smith (New York: Charles Scribner's Sons, 1958), p. 3.

7. *Ibid.*, p. 11.

8. Gabriel Marcel, *The Mystery of Being, 1. Reflection and Mystery*, trans. by G. S. Fraser, Gateway Edition (Chicago: Henry Regnery Company, 1960; originally published in Great Britain in 1950 by The Harvill Press, Ltd.).

9. Alfred Stern, *Sartre, His Philosophy and Psychoanalysis* (New York: The Liberal Arts Press, 1953), p. 126.

10. William Barrett, *Irrational Man* (Garden City: Doubleday and Company, 1958), p. 232.

11. Betty Friedan, *The Feminine Mystique* (New York: W. W. Norton and Company, 1963); see especially chap. 4.

12. See, for instance, my own "Male, Female, and the Higher Learning," *Journal of Higher Education*, Vol. XXX, No. 2 (February, 1959), pp. 67–72.

13. Stern, *op. cit.*, p. 126.

14. *Ibid.*

15. Jean-Paul Sartre, *Existentialism*, trans. by B. Frechtman (New York: Philosophical Library, 1947), p. 61.

4

ℰXISTENTIALISM AND THE

SCIENTIFIC PHILOSOPHIES

The foregoing account of basic Existential ideas is obviously not likely to mean much to the scientific mind. The philosophers of science—the Experimentalists and Positivists*—are used to a logic

* I am taking the liberty in this chapter of lumping together Positivists, logical empiricists, symbolic logicians, and ordinary language analysts. I am well aware of their intramural differences. Also, not all of them are "scientific philosophers," with whom I associate them. Nevertheless, it seems to me unarguable that there is a pole of thinking around which they

that finds little expression here. Some of them in my presence have dismissed it as "mere poetry."[1]

Although this is probably not the general view, still, there does seem to be a strategic idealogical schism now developing in twentieth-century philosophy which has reached what many of us consider serious proportions. Is some kind of rapprochement at all possible? Perhaps. An analysis of the schism itself might conceivably show the way, if not to a reunion in philosophy, at least to a sensible and mutually agreeable "division of labor" in philosophical inquiry. It is this possibility we will now explore.

THE ANATOMY OF DISAGREEMENT

We may begin at the outer edges of the difficulty by noting a commonplace, namely, that there has always been a certain tension between the scientific and the humanistic tempers. C. P. Snow, by now a household word among intellectuals, has rephrased the problem as one of garbled communication between the "two cultures" in contemporary thought. I suspect, however, that the communication breakdown originates merely in the fact that the sciences and the humanities ask essentially different kinds of questions about the world.

If you study man by the method suited to chemistry, or even if you study him in the light of what you have learned about rats and dogs, it is certainly to be expected that what you discover will be what chemistry and animal behavior have to teach. But it is also not surprising or even significant if by such methods you fail to discover anything else.[2]

It should be obvious, to scientist and humanist alike, that what

---

and the Experimentalists tend to gather; that this pole might be thought of as the interpretive variations, of admittedly differing intensity and relevance, which are rung on the theme of the "verifiability principle," and that this pole, however nebulous and impossible of exact definition, can be distinguished from the pole around which Existentialist thinkers do their work.

you find out about man and the world depends on the kinds of questions you ask. As Krutch concludes, ". . . the experimenter, the instruments he uses and the hypotheses which he adopts, are all parts of the experiment and help determine the results."[3] This is understatement, for the hypothesis one adopts does a lot more than "help." It determines *absolutely*, not the answer one will get, but the *kind* of answer that can be gotten. A question in the behavioral sciences concerning adolescents' attitudes cannot possibly issue in an answer concerning what their attitudes ought to be; a Toynbeean analysis of "civilization's highest values" in a tenth-grade civics class cannot possibly result in an answer that will explain how people actually live.

If the kind of question asked makes a difference, we are required to move to the next level of our problem and to inquire: What kinds of questions is it legitimate and proper to ask? The Positivists have developed a straightforward policy on this matter, a policy which can be worked out from the analysis of language itself. The very structure of our questions, they contend, can tell us whether or not they are legitimate. Specifically, the structure of the question must indicate the means by which it is to be answered. Any question which does not provide promising leads to its own solution— that is to say, any question which does not provide its own "rules of evidence" or grounds for what shall stand for proof—is outlawed as meaningless.

The fact that Positivists, with this argument, are asking questions about questions, and are therefore subject to their own rules, deserves out attention a little later. For now, let us merely note that their position invites some interesting comparisons:

Vision offers us an accurate analogy. It may be that I cannot see except by the use of spectacles. But to take off one pair of spectacles and to study them by another pair will not enable me to gain a panoramic view. It merely gives me another object to be fitted into such a view. . . . Analytical philosophy, which surrenders objective insight to focus on the logical and linguistic tools of knowledge, is like a man who becomes so interested in the cracks and spots of dust upon his glasses that he loses all interest in what he may actually see through them.[4]

IS EXISTENCE A PREDICATE?

By way of probing even closer to the heart of our problem, let us consider one of the Positivist's favorite arguments, namely, whether the word "existence" (or "being") has any meaning. Sooner or later, all analytic disputes gather in the vicinity of this question.

The word "existence" (or "being") is, by common consent, the "biggest" word in the philosopher's lexicon. It is therefore by far the most interesting spot of dust on the Positivist's spectacles. Can the word be said to mean anything? On the answer to this question hangs the outcome of the ideological struggle between Positivism and Existentialism.

If we are to take the advice of Sidney Hook, the answer must be a flat "No." In a well-known article Professor Hook argues at great length that Existential thinkers like Tillich, Heidegger, and Hartmann have really added very little to our understanding of the word "being."[5] He acknowledges, of course, that the word is common enough in our language and that it appears to have some limited meaning in ordinary speech.

The question is, however, whether the word "being" has any meaning in a philosophical context, and by a philosophical context I mean any activity which inquires into the logic and the procedures by which knowledge is built up and described.[6]

Interpreting the definition of "philosophical context" in this way, he comes to the conclusion that "being" does not belong in philosophy. All he is willing to assert is that the word "being" functions sometimes as an "infinity or zero word," i.e., a word which stands for some presupposed, ineffable, undefinable ground or context in which discourse takes place. Thus, words like "everything," "world," "universe," and "being" stand for that which is only implicitly present; what they stand for cannot be talked about or discussed.

The word "exist," he claims, suffers from the same affliction. As Kant made clear, it is not a true predicate or attribute or property like, say, "triangular" or "human." Triangularity may be a trait which we can assign to certain figures, but we would not say that existence is a "trait" which we can assign to entities in the world. To do so is to use language improperly.

Apropos Hook's point, Bertrand Russell's well-known Theory of Descriptions deserves inspection. A "description" is a phrase of the general sort, "the so-and-so," e.g., "the present President of the United States." According to the Theory, when a proposition containing such a phrase is properly analyzed, the phrase, "the so-and-so," disappears. Thus, the sentence "The golden mountain does not exist" really means: "There is no entity c such that 'x is golden and mountainous' is true when x is c."

Russell contends that one can only assert "existence" of descriptions.[7] Thus, we can say "The present President of the United States exists" because the description can be analyzed into the form: There is an entity c such that 'x is currently President of the United States' is true when x is c. But we cannot say "Lyndon Johnson exists" because, not being similarly analyzable, such a proposition is merely bad syntax, void of meaning.

But perhaps descriptions submit to the predicate "exist" for reasons other than their purely syntactical role in our propositions. Professor Frank B. Ebersole has undertaken a thoroughly analytic re-examination of the word "existence" and has some interesting things to say about it. Suppose, he writes, that I am a foreigner traveling through California and that "in my home town all we had heard of oranges was what a well-known teller of tall tales had said. Now I might write and say 'The fabulous orange we heard so much about exists.' "[8] What is wrong with that? Nothing at all; it is a perfectly sensible and intelligible use of "exist" as a predicate. Or consider another situation: A lawyer has built an elaborate case and someone shows him a letter that destroys his argument. Pondering the letter, he says, " 'I had no way of knowing that this letter existed, but it does.' "[9] Nothing wrong with that either. Finally, bring to mind, say, a little-known limited edition book published in 1849. "Rattle off these possibilities: 'All copies are red,' 'No copies are red,' 'Some copies are not red.' Now consider 'All copies exist,' 'Most copies do not exist,' etc."[10] Nothing wrong here either.

These and many other illustrations Professor Ebersole employs in his analysis. What, he asks, do we learn from this effort? "This much: one cannot tell that a sentence is nonsense by staring at the sentence. So one cannot tell whether existence is or is not a predicate by staring at sentences containing the word 'exists' in one position or another."[11] One can tell only by considering the situation in which the sentence is uttered and thus the occasion for using the word "exist." To say that something exists and to be understood merely requires "a special kind of background."[12] It may be true that there is a difference between the predicate "exist" and such predicates as "triangular" or "green" or "tall." But "if this difference . . . is indeed there, it is still a long way from the difference between predicate and nonpredicate."[13]

On his own ground, then, the logical empiricist may have difficulty nailing down his own argument. But, on review, there is an even more profound fault in the empiricist's position. When Professor Hook insists that "a philosophical context" means "any activity which inquires into the logic and the procedures by which knowledge is built up and described," he makes the mistake of thinking that "the logic and the procedures" all have to do with knowledge of the objective world. All of his examples, and indeed all of Professor Ebersole's examples, concern the existence of entities in the world *other than myself*. As we have pointed out earlier (see Chapter 1, page 19), these annoying problems of the word "exist" never intrude on my understanding of my own presence in the world. And it is in this awareness that the predication of existence makes all the difference.

Professor Hook chides Tillich and Heidegger for concocting "purely psychological categories" when speaking of being and nonbeing. But that is just the point. If existence and nothingness are psychological categories, then so much the worse for whatever other kinds of categories there may be in the world. Isn't it sensible to suppose that the awarenesses we have directly—of our own existence, or of our possible nonexistence—are somehow as genuinely meaningful as sensations of objects outside our own bodies? (Professor Hook's implied disdain for the "purely psychological" is the type of attitude George Santayana was protesting when he remarked, "Man has a prejudice against himself: anything which is a product of his mind seems to him to be unreal or comparatively insignificant."[14])

William Barrett sums up the matter this way:

> . . . *all modern Positivism takes its cue from Kant's doctrine and discards all thinking about existence . . . as pointless because existence cannot be represented in a concept. . . . The crossroad in modern philosophy is precisely here, and [Existentialism] takes a road leading in the opposite direction from that taken by Positivism. If existence cannot be represented in a concept, . . . it is not because it is too general, remote, and tenuous a thing to be conceived of but rather because it is too dense, concrete, and rich. I am; and this fact that I exist is so compelling and enveloping a reality that it cannot be reduced thinly in any of my mental concepts. . . .*[15]

> *My existence is not a mental representation but a fact in which I am plunged up to the ears, and indeed over the head.*[16]

The reluctance of empirical and positivistic philosophies to take existence seriously stems, of course, from the fact that existential phenomena—e.g., awareness, feelings, anguish in its many forms—do not yield to a scientific logic. Such phenomena are therefore deemed unworthy of inclusion in serious philosophical discourse. There is a certain irony to this dismissal, since the scientific philosophies, Pragmatism in particular, have always argued that what they are attempting to do is to turn philosophy away from the arid technicalities of classical metaphysics toward consideration of the living problems of real people. Yet the *most real* experiences of real people, those we may now classify as existential, are somehow not accepted for consideration.

> [This attitude] *may be indicated by an example, slight in itself but suggestive of a larger contrast. Death is certainly an important fact in every man's life; look at the way in which . . . a pragmatist like Dewey treat[s] it. In the course of his argument against the traditional means-end conception in* Human Nature and Conduct, *Dewey analyzes the situation of a man building a house. The man is not building the house in order to live in it, Dewey says, for he might die before it was finished; so he is building it for the sake of the present activity itself.*[17]

The careful student of Dewey will certainly find this last sentence a questionable oversimplification of the means-ends relationship in his philosophy. Yet, the larger point Miss Grene is making still holds, namely, that Dewey's interest was almost exclusively directed to the understanding of means and ends in the routines of daily living. He was not interested in the more profound, and ultimately more human problem posed by the end toward which every man is committed—death.

THE VERIFIABILITY CRITERION
OF MEANING

To press the "spectacles" simile a trifle, we may say that the Positivist has been looking at specks and spots of dust so long and with such singleness of purpose that they seem to him the only real things. But this is not all. He has overlooked the possibility that his own criterion of meaning—the so-called "verifiability principle"—may conceivably be one of the spots. When this criterion is turned upon itself, we witness an interesting result.

The verifiability principle can be stated somewhat as follows: To be meaningful, a proposition must be such either (1) that it is true by definition (as is the case with analytic tautologies) or (2) that some possible sense experience would be relevant to the determination of its truth. (The latter kind of proposition is usually called "synthetic.") If a proposition fails to meet this criterion, it is literally senseless. According to the test, the following propositions are all meaningless or, as we say, noncognitive:

The intellect naturally tends to know.
Moral laws are embedded in reality.
Existence precedes essence.
X exists.
I exist.

Does the verifiability principle itself belong in the list? To answer this question, we must scrutinize the principle—as the Positivist recommends for all propositions—to determine its exact status. Is it a tautology? Apparently not; the predicate is not analyzed out of meanings already contained in the subject. Is it synthetic? Apparently not; there would not appear to be any sense experience relevant to the establishment of its truth or falsity. Hence, we must reluctantly add it to the Positivist's list of meaningless, noncognitive propositions.

The Positivist usually rejoins by saying that his principle is merely a "proposal." But a "mere" proposal is still a proposal and as such takes on a character which ironically the Positivist considers inferior to that of a cognitive statement.

To explain this last, we may adopt the Positivist's own reasoning: The noncognitive statements listed above must be relegated to the category of "emotive" statements, i.e., statements that tell us nothing about the world, but only how the speaker feels at the moment. As it happens, a "proposal" falls into this classification; it is a statement which recommends something, a statement of preference. The verifiability principle is indeed a proposal! It tells us nothing about what is actually the case concerning logic or the use of language. It tells us only that the speaker *wants* us to use language in a prescribed way. As such, the principle is just as emotive as any statement of preference. What the principle is really saying is this: "One *ought* to consider meaningful only that proposition which . . ."

It should now be plain that how one *ought* to decide on the meaningfulness of language is a long way from saying how one *must* decide on the meaningfulness of language. And this brings us to the very heart of our difficulty.

THE CRUX: IS REASON ITS OWN "OUGHT"?

The usual counter to the above line of argument is that there is an implied "must" in the use of language, that, to be rational, we must use language in a certain way if the human enterprise in general and philosophy in particular are to succeed. What good is language if there are no rules by which it can be made rational instead of simply poetic or inspirational or demagogic or fatuous (to consider just a few stops on the descending, emotive continuum)?

And to be rational is what being human is all about. As the Experimentalists have often put it: Man has an obligation to be intelligent.[18]

Now, what does this mean? It must mean that intelligence is something I automatically owe to the world. But the paradox is that, if I automatically owe it, then I cannot *choose* to owe it to the world. I cannot voluntarily assume the obligation to be intelligent; it is already "written into" the nature of things. And if it is somehow "written in," then it cannot be a *good* since it cannot be freely chosen.

There is a curious resistance to this notion, voiced by people who seem to think that intelligence (or reason) can be, at one and the same time, both automatically given as an object of allegiance *and* a free option which is merely one of man's possibilities. The Positivists, for example, take for granted man's desire to be intelligent and rational in his discourse.

But there have been more sophisticated attempts to establish reason as both *given* and *possible* as a value in the world. One comes from Professor Harry Broudy, who, although not a Positivist, puts it in a way that some Positivists might find agreeable:

. . . the recognition that one can be rational generates the duty to be rational, i.e., we have here an "is" that generates its own "ought," for even if one could conclude that one ought not to be reasonable in a particular situation, it could be justified only on grounds that this is a reasonable conclusion.[19]

The difficulty in this position lies in the seeming urgency to establish a self-justifying Prime Value. Like the ancient metaphysicians who searched in vain for the Prime Mover or First Cause, Broudy seeks a Prime Value which is somehow its own justification. The price one must pay for this kind of thinking comes in two denominations: First, the argument offers us a notion of self-causation or self-generation which is as unacceptable as the notion of an Uncaused Causer or Prime Mover was to an earlier age. Second, and more important, by establishing a self-justifying value, the argument succeeds in destroying the value itself. A self-justifying value is a contradiction in terms! How can I value something which is required of me by the world? Or, as Sartre once put it,

"[If] certain values exist prior to me, it is self-contradictory for me to want them and at the same [time] state that they are imposed on me."[20]

Hence, to use plain language, if reason is self-justifying, it cannot possibly be a value. This is the real explanation for the dictum that from an "is" there issues no "ought." Any "is" cannot be chosen; it is already there. Only when something *is* chosen can it be converted into a value. A "given" cannot be chosen; only "possibles" can be chosen, and thus turned into goods. A thing cannot be both given *and* possible; hence it cannot be both given *and* valuable. The breach remains between the "is" and the "ought." It is an absolute breach.

Once again, Barrett's powers of summary are very helpful:

Contrary to the rationalist tradition, we now know that it is not his reason that makes man man, but rather that reason is a consequence of that which really makes him man. For it is man's existence as a self-transcending self that has forged and formed reason as one of its projects.[21]

It is precisely because the free self of man has opted for reason that reason can be called a value. One has to *choose* to be rational, and if it were not for that fact, being rational would not be a value but merely a brute necessity in the world.

Man, therefore, is better defined not as a rational animal but as a *choosing*, and therefore valuing, animal who *can* think and *does* think if he chooses. Because it is grounded in man's existing, choosing precedes reasoning. Man *must* choose; there is no escaping choice. Man *may* reason if he chooses. Hence, choosing and therefore valuing are both ontologically and psychologically prior to reason. Man may share reason or intelligence with other organisms; he is simply better at it than they. But man stands alone as a *valuer*; he apparently shares this predicate with no other entity in the world.

One way to illuminate this notion might be to ask a few very homely questions of ourselves: Which is the more noble, more distinctly human specimen, the reasoning man or the valuing man? Or, to make the contrast complete and thoroughgoing, even if obviously artificial, let us ask: Who is the more eligible to be called human, the man of reason incapable of valuing or the valuing man incapable of reason? Admittedly these are preposterous prototypes, but they point up the distinction which, analytically at least, must be made. And there is no question as to which man the Existentialist understands as the more eligible. Our sense of value in the world is certainly a higher, more distinctively, exclusively, and uniquely *human* quality than any amount of rationality.

To put it in more personal terms, we might ask it this way: Suppose you were to lose either your reason or your power to choose between good and evil? Which would you rather lose? On the one hand, you could picture yourself as a thoroughly sophisticated thinking machine, capable of every known rational operation but completely incapable of distinguishing between right and wrong. On the other hand, you could imagine yourself completely involved in the moral dimension of the world, concerned with the advance of right over wrong, good over bad, personally responsible for the furtherance of values in the world, but incapable of even the most childish mental operations. In which of these two admittedly outlandish paradigms can we recognize a residual trace, the last remainder, so to speak, of the human? No need to temporize about this; the *latter* man would be the clear option of the Existentialist.

I think this declaration can be put in even more prosaic but possibly more poignant terms: Which is the more human, to have a mind "like a steel trap" or to have a sensitive compassion for good? Which is the more inhuman fault, to be unthinking or to be unfeeling? To the Existentialist, the latter is unquestionably worse.

DÉTENTE AND DIVISION OF PHILOSOPHIC LABOR

The foregoing argument does *not* mean to suggest that reason is to be demoted to some limbo of insignificance. Quite the contrary—and we must say it again, lest there be any misconstruction of this point—reason is to be sought out and advocated as a *good* precisely because man has freely chosen it as one of his projects in the world. What has elevated reason to the rank of a value is the very fact that man has chosen it as one of his modes of expression. What we must guard against is the notion that it is his *only* mode of expression, the only legitimate vehicle through which to exhibit his humanness. A few paragraphs back attention was drawn to a common assumption of contemporary scientific philosophy, viz., "to be rational is what being human is all about." The Existentialist has no desire to repeal this. He merely wants to qualify and rephrase it: "To be rational is *one possibility* of the human enterprise." There are, after all, other possibilities.

We value reason and intelligence and the exercise of thought upon the world's work not because these ingredients are written into our nature; we value them because they have been freely appropriated by this free being called man. Reason is a human *project*. It is a grand hypothesis as to the *meaning of man*. We are, as it were, engaged in a trial of this hypothesis to see if it really is all there is to being human. It is only a possible, not a foregone, conclusion that "rational" = "human." Man's project in reason, his project in trying-to-be-intelligent, is an attempt to decide on the legitimacy of the equals sign.

But another point must be made clear. In order for this project to have any significance, it must be a freely appropriated undertaking. To strike out on the adventure of reason as a tentative possibility for the meaning of man is to say that the outcome is not certain. (I am not referring to the outcome of whether man can succeed at being intelligent, but to the outcome of whether intelligence and rationality represent what the human enterprise means in the world.) To assume the "obligation to be intelligent" is, therefore, to make a choice which is arbitrary, unjustified, and unfounded. This does not mean that one is not entitled to make it. It means only that it is a choice for which no further grounds can be given; there are no criteria of a higher rank or a more general magnitude by which such a choice could be justified.

And that is precisely what makes reason and intelligence worth pursuing. As free and unjustified projects, they represent a value which has been created and introduced into the world by man.

Man, not the world, is responsible for there being a value entitled "reason" in place in the universe. But, like all value, its tenure is precarious for it can always be opted against, disvalued, and driven out; man can always decide against it.

Which is to say that man has *another* project running concurrently. It vies with "rationality" as the real meaning of the human enterprise. It is the project in assessing the significance of man as *chooser*, rather than man as thinker. It goes without saying that this project is, by definition, partly concerned with the noncognitive and emotive. Man is, in effect, trying out various arational, nonrational (or however one wants to put it) meanings for man. He is exploring various spheres of noncognitive *awareness*, to see what possibilities for human feeling may conceivably deserve attention. And these too are arbitrary, unfounded options for which no justification can be given.

The point is that we do not know for sure what the human enterprise is *for* in the world. We do not know what we individually are *for*. And an interest in this question cannot be dismissed just because it sounds Aristotelian; it cannot be dismissed so long as it is a problem every man faces. The alternate projects, in *reason* or in *awareness*, are tentative explorations of what we are for in the world. Further, they are not being undertaken by some abstract entity called "man." They are being undertaken by each one of us in our own lives. Each life is a project to determine the meaning of man. Each individual must choose what he wants his life to say concerning man's definition in the world. Each individual shapes an answer to this question in terms of what he chooses to devote his life to.

And this brings us to the ground for a détente between different kinds of philosophers, for they, *as individual persons*, have chosen different intellectual careers, different life projects. They have committed their lives to different arbitrary spheres of effort. They have, in effect, declared with their lives their own definition of man as they see it. Can we agree on this much?

If so, the *choice to be rational*, having been taken by the philosophers of science, can now be exploited. They will tell us just how we are to be most effectively rational in our discourse. Along this path most certainly lies the analysis of language, an analysis which is completely justified on the basis of the prior value, the choice to be rational, already declared. But if the choice to be rational is without justification itself (and it must be in order to retain its status as a value), then other choices in other directions, also unjustified and unfounded and arbitrary, can just as legitimately be exploited for their possible meaning and significance for the human enterprise. It is along these lines that the exploration of existential phenomena—the awareness of death, the anguish of nothingness, each man's private management of the existential paradox—would appear to lie. Recognizing this, can we agree, therefore, to let each arbitrary choice of what shall be declared "human" be developed in its own way.

What I am trying to say is this: Each philosopher appropriates for his own career a certain sector of intellectual exploration; he marks out, is it were, certain problems which he calls *his*. Thus he makes an arbitrary value judgment. The very act of addressing oneself to a problem is to declare that so using one's life is a good thing to do. To undertake the study of certain problems is itself a judgment that a human being *ought* to be concerned with these problems.

To become interested in logical and linguistic analysis, to examine its methods and procedures, to think and write about it, is to argue for its importance in life. It is to select it out of all that there may be for men to do, to bracket it against the background of all the other things men find worth doing, and to say that this is what we *ought* to spend our time on. I, for one, do not begrudge this effort of the language analysts to help us be clear in our thinking. Indeed, I admire it, all the more because I find it uninspiring to engage in it myself. My passion for clarity is not as well developed as theirs, but I am glad there are people who are so passionate.

But keep in mind that it is a passion, just as mine for other kinds of philosophizing may be. And no one need apologize for passion; it is one's way of looking at the world and deciding where one's energies should go and therefore what one's life is for.

So may we let the philosophers of science pursue their arbitrary passion for the scientifically cognitive, for the linguistically logical and rational. And may we let the Existentialist pursue his arbitrary passion for the personally cognitive and also for the noncognitive, emotive, and normative.

Man's meaning in the world has not been finally determined.

NOTES

1. Since poetry deals with the world in connotative rather than denotative language, it is said to have no strictly cognitive meaning. What kind of meaning it *does* have is still an open question.
2. Joseph Wood Krutch, *The Measure of Man* (Indianapolis: The Bobbs-Merrill Company, 1953), p. 105.
3. *Ibid.*, p. 106.
4. John Wild, *The Challenge of Existentialism* (Bloomington: Indiana University Press, 1959), p. 10.
5. Sidney Hook, "The Quest for 'Being,'" *Journal of Philosophy*, Vol. L, No. 24 (November 19, 1953). This article eventually grew into a book, *The Quest for Being, and Other Studies in Naturalism and Humanism* (New York: St. Martin's Press, 1961).
6. *Ibid.*, p. 719 (italics in the original).
7. Bertrand Russell, *Introduction to Mathematical Philosophy* (London: George Allen and Unwin, Ltd., 1919), pp. 178–179.
8. Frank B. Ebersole, "Whether Existence Is a Predicate," *Journal of Philosophy*, Vol. LX, No. 18 (August 29, 1963), p. 510.
9. *Ibid.*, p. 516.
10. *Ibid.*, p. 517.
11. *Ibid.*
12. *Ibid.*, p. 511.
13. *Ibid.*
14. *The Sense of Beauty* (New York: Charles Scribner's Sons, 1896), p. 3.
15. William Barrett, *Irrational Man* (Garden City: Doubleday and Company, 1958), p. 144.
16. *Ibid.*, p. 264.
17. Marjorie Grene, *Dreadful Freedom* (Chicago: University of Chicago Press, 1948), p. 26.
18. For the sake of this discussion, I am using "reason," "rationality," and "intelligence" as more or less interchangeable.

Existentialism as a Philosophy

19. Harry S. Broudy, "Reply to D. B. Gowin," *Studies in Philosophy and Education*, Vol. II (Winter, 1961–1962), p. 49.

20. Jean-Paul Sartre, *Existentialism*, trans. by B. Frechtman (New York: Philosophical Library, 1947), p. 53.

21. Barrett, *op. cit.*, p. 247.

part two Existentialism in education

5

$\mathcal{A}$N EDUCATIONAL THEORY

THE HAZARDS OF APPLICATION

We move now to the educational meaning of the foregoing set of ideas. Can an Existential analysis of the human condition suggest any lines of argument for the education of the young?

The answer is "Yes." But the development of this answer in the final two chapters will persuade nobody unless notice is taken of some severe caveats which other investigators have expressed concerning the all too easy fitting together of philosophical and educational notions. Our discussion of Existentialist theory in education may appropriately open by acknowledging and answering these demurrers. The caveats take several different forms.

Perhaps the most sweeping is the argument that nothing educational follows logically from that which is philosophical. This is the line of the Positivist, and I think he means that nothing political or social or moral or aesthetic follows either. That is to say, philosophy can tell us nothing about how to organize a civilization, run a society, or live a single human life. All it can tell us is how to talk, i.e., how to use our language properly and correctly.

There is a curious fault in this argument: Just why is it that the way we talk is properly open to philosophical criticism but the way we live is not? Is not talking part of living? If philosophy cannot instruct us on the direction of human affairs, individual or social, how is it possible for philosophy to instruct us on the use of language, which is one of the most exclusively human of all affairs? Positivists have decided that the old metaphysical principles lead nowhere because they are somehow beyond the pale of the "verifiable" in human experience. And they are right.

But how verifiable is their own principle of verifiability? As pointed out in the previous chapter, the proof of this principle is as far beyond the pale of the "verifiable" as anything that an Idealist or Realist ever uttered. Just why is it improper to use language in certain ways? Who says it is improper? And if the answer is that improper language yields propositions which are not verifiable, who is being so presumptuous as to say that only verifiable propositions should pass beyond my teeth? Who now is playing God?

The Positivists are entitled to their own metaphysical presuppositions, of which the verifiability principle is Number One. But we must convince the Positivists that it is indeed a metaphysical presupposition, enjoying no higher rank than presuppositions supporting other persuasions.

If, therefore, philosophy is to be given the privilege of criticizing my talk, I see no reason why it should not also be given the privilege of criticizing my understanding of the world, the way I shape the pattern of my life, and the possibilities I see for educating the young.

Another objection, of somewhat the same genre, is directed more specifically at Existentialism. It is argued, again by the Positivist, that Existentialist notions are unverifiable not so much in the traditional metaphysical sense, i.e., lying beyond the world of experience, as for almost the opposite reason, namely, that they are only privately and subjectively "felt" and cannot be verified by the open community. In a certain sense, this charge may be correct. But all it can mean is that a prior value judgment has already been made, viz., that the *community* criterion has some kind of ultimate superiority over the *individual* criterion in deciding how life is to be looked at. It means that a view of life is defensible only after it has passed through the "public square" and been gawked at and judged by the impersonal crowd.

But this is the whole point: If Existentialism seems to many people to originate in what we might call a "psychological metaphysics" (e.g., "I exist." "Existence precedes essence."), then so much the worse for whatever other kinds of metaphysics there may be, *including* the as yet unnamed metaphysics supporting the verifiability principle. Existentialism dares to assert that the so-called "uncoerced community of persuasion," for all its high-sounding, moral scientism, cannot ever become the final judge of how I look at life and how I live it. If the community persuasion is to be such an arbiter, I as an individual must actively consent to it, *choose* it, as my life's arbiter.

In practical terms: If in the privacy of my own subjectivity I feel certain feelings, if I have certain awarenesses which to me are authentic and laden with personal meaning for my own project, I do not need a linguistic philosopher to tell me whether I should or should not allow these awarenesses to flow into my teaching of the young on the ground that they cannot be completely shared by the community. Must an awareness become public property in order to be human? The question is ridiculous on its face. In the I-Thou relationship which the Existentialist sees prevailing between teacher and learner, awarenesses wither under the glare of publicity; they are destroyed by becoming the playthings of group dynamics and sociometry. The *group*, for all its cognitive, problem-solving capabilities in educational situations, cannot ever completely tune to that frequency of interhuman communication which is affective and emotional in character.

The above argument may now be expanded to typify a third and, to some, decisive demurrer to Existentialism as a possible philosophy of education. It is argued that education as we have come to know it is, by historical function and genetic structure, a *social* undertaking. It would be impossible, the objectors allege, to understand education at all unless it were viewed as the institutional expression of some culture in a given time and place, an organized effort to perpetuate itself in history. This culturological frame for education has been made popular by the Experimentalists, and their suspicion is that since Existentialism grows out of a private, "psychological metaphysics" it is incapable of developing anything that could be called a sociology. And without a sociology no philosophy can hope to construct an educational theory.[1]

Here again, the charge has something more than mere plausibility to it. Existentialism certainly is *not* well known for its literature in social science. Nevertheless, I think something constructive can be said in answer to the charge.

In his book *Escape from Freedom*[2] Erich Fromm develops a theme which, although by now commonplace among social psychologists, can be instructive to us because it sets the Existential predicament in its commonest terms and makes possible a sociological analogy. He says that individuals are frequently in anguish over the baselessness of their values; freedom is simply too much for them; they cannot stand a life without directions, sanctions, laws, and ethical principles handed down from on high. Hence, they try to "escape" this condition by submitting to external (that is, external to their own will) determinants of conduct.

The most brutal and vicious examples of this are the Fascist and Communist totalitarianisms of the twentieth century. But, lest an overwhelming self-righteousness set in, we must remember that Americans too are caught in the grip of the same vise. They still harbor a nostalgia for a final sanction to their lives, an ideology that will give shape and point to their existence, an "American ethic" to repair to and identify with.

Consider the recent pleadings in our country to identify a "national purpose." The pulpits, the mass media, the pundits and political moralists all took great delight in addressing themselves to this theme during the late 1950s and early 1960s. With rolling, ponderous prose our scriveners and orators tried desperately to utter quotable quotes that would ring down the ages. (Those who spoke most ponderously probably felt the need of a national ideology more than those who listened.) The excitement such a question can generate among our moral leaders tells us something about ourselves. Our frantic search for a national ideology—is this not a group request for some grand purpose to certify and give warrant to our present national conduct? And is this not, on a mass, sociological scale, an analogous instance of our corporate "escape from freedom"?

The Existentialist understandably sickens at the sight of this lemming-like craving for national guidance, for a "group think" credential that will explain to the world why Americans are as they are. The Existentialist counterreply on social and political questions would therefore appear to be something like this: If the authentic man is our aim, then the authentic society is also our aim. That society is authentic in the degree to which it fails to provoke in the individual citizen these urgings to escape from his freedom. That society is authentic which refuses to specify "the good" to its citizens. That society is authentic in the degree to which it summons the citizen to stand by himself, for himself, in shaping the direction of his life, and therefore the meaning of his existence. That society is authentic which never achieves a "national purpose," which is, in fact, uninterested in achieving one, but interested only in being the host to individual purposes in its citizens.

Is such a society possible? Who can say? Can a society emerge in which each individual takes *personal* responsibility for the laws he obeys, the conventions he consents to, the values he appropriates for his own life? Whatever it may take to answer these questions is what I shall be calling an Existential sociology. And I think a theory of education can be understandable in these terms.

But at a deeper level, is a sociology all that vital to an educational theory? Just what counts as a sociology? The trouble may lie in giving too literal an interpretation to the word "social." Man is a social animal, yes, but perhaps only because of his physical proximity to organisms of his own kind. Such a primitive conception of "sociality" really says nothing about the *attitude* he is forced to adopt toward the other organisms. This *attitude* is open for discussion, and only at the close of the discussion can the attitude, generalized into common understandings, be called a social theory or sociology. Hence, if education is an activity that is carried on with young people *in groups,* this does not preclude the possibility of considering students in groups physically only; psychologically, they may still be understood as subjectivities existing alone as individuals. It is the latter aspect of human growth and development that can rightfully become the subject matter of an Existentialist theory of education, whether or not some putative sociology has already been worked out.

We may conclude this procedural forenote by insisting that Existentialism does not argue its way into educational philosophy merely by offering a rebuttal to various objections. Its real case is made by what it has positively to offer. If, as a philosophy, it begins with a question and ends with a question, let us make the most of the questions.

Man has been "thrown into the world," he has "turned up in the world." Where or when is only of archeological or historical interest. The FACT is that *man has turned up.* Here he is. The question is, Why? What significance is to be attached to the coming into the world of a being who is, alone among all beings, *aware* of his very awareness and hence uniquely capable of asking himself *why* he is?

> The problem which [Existentialism] poses is a seemingly elementary one: Is not man, thrown into a world which he did not create, confronted with obligations of a communal existence, forced to comply with the imperatives of an anonymous society, and continually faced with the inevitability of his own death—is not man, so conceived, incapable of justifying his own existence?[3]

If the answer to this question seems to be "Yes," the puzzle is that man doesn't believe his own answer! He goes on trying to unravel the mystery of his "why" in the face of his cognitive comprehension of the fact that it cannot be unraveled. He cannot shut the haunting question from his mind, and at the same time he cannot seem to accept the answer given to him by reason. And it is in this blatant thrust beyond reason, this unconquerable, inquisitive expedition which shoots free of mere cognition, that he invades and marks out the particular zone which he creates for himself and which makes him human, the zone where values are created in the act of an individual living a life.

To encourage the young to invade this zone and stake out their own plots there—this is an Existentialist education.

DOES EDUCATION HAVE A DEFINITION?

It is a convention in the craft that every philosophy is expected to concoct and offer up a grand, plenary, umbrella-like phrase under which all lesser educational ideas are to be classified and understood. The world of educational philosophy has its full share of these final, all-embracing rubrics.

One of the oldest and still the most popular is the notion that education is the drawing out of our common human nature. The Aristotelian Rational Humanists and the Neo-Thomists in general, and Robert Hutchins and Mortimer Adler in particular, have made this a virtual byword slogan in twentieth-century educational philosophy. Working from a supposed etymological root of the word "education" in the Latin *educere*, "to lead out," they insist that all education is a process of summoning forth prior but only incipient elements in the child's nature. As it happens, there is considerable disagreement about this etymology among Latin scholars; some claim that "education" comes from *educare*, "to rear or nurture." Although the latter view might provide the base for a differently oriented definition, in either case education is thought of as working with what is already given in the child's nature.

A somewhat less sophisticated and more prosaic definition of education is the taking on, or the "taking *in*," of the accumulated and stored-up knowledge and wisdom of the race. This view, generally attributed to those who call themselves Essentialists, has been espoused by the late William C. Bagley and the contemporary Clifton Hall. The child is a passive element in a process by which he receives, absorbs, and assimilates the various arts and sciences of civilization. Professor Hall speaks of it as "furnishing the mind," an expression intended, I think, to call forward the analogy of furnishing an apartment.[4] No prior nature is postulated except the capacity (the "container" metaphor is intentional) to receive and be the receptacle for as much of the world's knowledge as possible, and, of course, in the process to develop the major skills of reading, writing, and calculating upon which all such learning depends.

According to a third definition, more nearly tuned to the behavioral sciences of the twentieth century and developed with some force by such individuals as George Counts and John Childs, education is the shaping of individuals—their understandings, their attitudes, their values and aspirations—in terms of the culture in which they happen to live. Here the assimilation of the arts and sciences of civilization is taken for granted. But which arts? Which sciences? The *use* to which the arts and sciences shall be put is always determined by a culture existing at a specific time in history and a specific place in the world's political geography. Hence, the *value* of this or that art or science is always a function of the social system at a given time in its history. Thus, whether or not a particular art or science is to be taught or learned is a negotiable matter to be determined in light of the culture's own ethic. As the famous epigram has it, whatever a culture values, that will it teach to its young. And that will its young become.

Finally, we may draw upon an even more general definition offered a half-century ago by John Dewey, a definition which does, in a sense, rationalize and make comprehensible all definitions of education which issue from philosophical origins. In a passage probably quoted more frequently than any other, especially by educational philosophers in justifying what they do for a living, Professor Dewey epitomizes the vital link between education and philosophy: "If we are willing to conceive education as the process of forming fundamental dispositions, intellectual and emotional, toward nature and fellow men, philosophy may even be defined *as the general theory of education.*"[5]

The latter portion of this passage has been worried over in endless commentaries in the field of philosophy of education. There is no need to discuss it further. Rather, I wish to draw attention to the definition of education made explicit in the first clause: "the process of forming fundamental dispositions." This is sufficiently straightforward not to require any labored exegesis, but perhaps a small gloss might be offered for it: Dewey is saying that human beings have dispositions ("intellectual and emotional, toward nature and fellow men"), that some of these dispositions are fundamental, that it is conceivable and possible to form them in young people by deliberate, intentional, and premeditated means, and that this activity we shall call by the name education.

Now, precisely what does it signify to speak of a disposition as being "fundamental"? Although there may be no strict logical entailment in such an equivalence, I think Dewey is clearly trying to intimate that whatever is fundamental is somehow desirable and worth pursuing in the process of "forming." He has given a kind of heuristic assignment to the word "fundamental" by which he implies that the dispositions to be formed are not only fundamental but of considerable interest to us; they are important to the task of giving a young person's developing life a focus and an orientation necessary for happiness and success. In short, we very much *want* youngsters to possess these dispositions.

Are we reading too much into the definition? I think not. A few pages prior to the passage quoted, Dewey speaks of the role of philosophy as "thinking what the known demands of us—what responsive attitude it exacts." And when he marries philosophy to education, it is clear that he expects some responsive attitudes to turn out to be of higher rank or of more lasting value than others. These are the attitudes to be formed.

To thus paraphrase Dewey does not mean to suggest that he is ignoring the important role of the learner. Indeed, most of Dewey's writing in education served to explain how this role could become far more active and constructive than any previous theory had conceived it. Not only was the child a participant in the "forming" activity but, through his own experience and the "feedback" effect of his reaction to the dispositions made available to him, the learner actively shared in deciding what dispositions were most worth forming in his own character. The fact remains, however, that the dispositions finally decided upon were not of his own unique authorship; they were always the dispositions that had been worked out in company with others. Hence, in the end, the learner discovered that he did not need to take *personal* responsibility for having selected them as the dispositions most suited to his own life. They were the dispositions worked out and certified by the group. They were not *his*.

One of the dispositions on which Dewey put a high value was

the disposition to *share*. The sharing of information, the sharing of experiences, the sharing of viewpoints and opinions, the sharing of cooperative help in the working out of learning projects—all these were considered good, and the disposition to share with one's fellows came to have an overpowering importance in Dewey's educational theory. Inevitably, the "morality of sharing" places a high premium on human intercourse and personal gregariousness. Gregariousness, then, came to assume a large auxiliary function in support of the sharing disposition. It is partly for this reason that, under Dewey's influence and that of the Progressives over the last fifty years, the *socialization* of the child has come into equal prominence with the *intellectual development* of the child as a strategic educational aim.

Now, here we have, from a variety that might have been cited, four representative and widely held definitions of education. The reader of this book should have no trouble detecting the flaw they all contain so far as an Existentialist educator might be concerned. Education may be all of these things superficially, he would say, but each viewpoint makes the same mistake, the mistake of believing that the young are *things* to be worked over in some fashion to bring them into alignment with a prior notion of what they *should* be. The young, in these conceptions of education, are to be *used*; they are to be employed on behalf of (1) a prepared, precertified idea of "human nature" which they are expected to fulfill, (2) an objective body of extant subject matter which they are expected to absorb, (3) an objective concept of a culture's ways and means of living which they are expected to assume, or (4) a set of dispositions, deemed fundamental, which are to be formed in them and for which they are expected to become the living vehicles.

In every case the process of education is understood to have its aim and point *outside* the learner. The child, by virtue of what is to be done with him and for him, is eventually seen as an object rather than a subject. His activity of learning is aroused and promoted in the name of considerations residing outside his own self-determination and self-direction.

I am not so naïve as to think that this charge will go unchallenged by Experimentalists and Progressives. As everyone knows, they claim to have succeeded, where earlier theories had not, in bringing the learner at last into a self-determining posture. It may come as some surprise to them, therefore, to hear someone say that they have failed to deliver on this pledge. But that is precisely what I am prepared to assert.

We have hinted at the difficulty in the paragraphs above dealing with Dewey's conception of education as "the forming of fundamental dispositions." Even if the child is a participant in the forming process, and even if he is in a cybernetic way always helping to decide what dispositions are most worth forming, it is still true in Experimentalist theory that the criterion he uses for judging one disposition against another will be a *public* rather than a personal and private criterion. That is to say, whether a disposition measures up as worthy of adoption will always be decided in terms of whether it will aid the individual in his present and future existence *with* and *among* other people. Under the aegis of an unspoken, virtually iron law of Experimentalist moral theory, a *public* criterion will always, in the last analysis, outrank and overpower a purely *private* criterion as to how life is to be looked at and lived.

I think we can see in the previously mentioned "uncoerced community of persuasion" the clue to the Achilles' heel of Experimentalist doctrine. The key word in this well-known phrase is *community*. Here, I think it not unfair to say, the Experimentalist finally rests his case. The *community* dimension to the Experimentalist's logic, to his method of inquiry, to his moral theory is the final, unarguable principle. As an article of doctrine, if not of faith, it is the ultimate canon which is not negotiable. If the test of the truth of an idea lies in its effects, these effects are understood to be *public* effects; if the test of a moral prescription lies in its consequences, these consequences are understood to be *public* consequences. Public effects and public consequences are the only kinds that can be useful to science. In the social sciences especially we see this requirement most vividly. Without public, repeatable phenomena, the social scientist's data would mean nothing. His data are, by definition, the data of purely public events.

It should surprise no one, then, that an Experimentalist's education has to be oriented to the public, community criterion. What is to be learned, how it is to be learned, how the learning of it is to be adjudged successful or unsuccessful—all these have their determination against a social measure. If this or that learning experience is made available to a youngster, in the final analysis its importance in his learning career will be argued for in terms of what it can mean for him in the *world of others*. What that experience may mean to him for purely private consumption will possibly intrude as an ancillary note, but in Experimentalist educational theory such a consideration is always, and indeed must be, subordinate.

In light of the foregoing argument we can see a disturbing truth, namely, that an Experimentalist definition of education eventually falters, like all the others, in its attempt to bring the learner's own self-determination to the very center of the learning process. And it is precisely this that Existentialism claims to do.

Does Existentialism have a definition of education? I am not so sure. There is a certain wariness of definitions in such a philosophy. Yet there is at least the possibility that something comprehensible can be put into words to typify the Existentialist's stance vis-à-vis the educative process. He might say something like this: If education is to be truly human, it must somehow *awaken awareness* in the learner—existential awareness of himself as a single subjectivity present in the world.

To be human is first to exist, and to exist is to be aware of being, to be aware of existing. This awareness is manifest most vividly, as we have said, in the awareness of choosing, the sometimes painful, sometimes exhilarating awareness of oneself as a baseless base of value creation. Is this "awareness," someone might ask, another of those "fundamental dispositions" which were just put aside a few pages back? The answer must be "No." How can awareness be a disposition? To be aware is not to be disposed this way or that. It is, rather, to be aware of the *possibility* of being disposed this way or that. *It is to be aware that one is the author of his own dispositions!*

To be disposed to sharing, one must *choose* to be so disposed. To be gregarious, one must individually *choose* gregariousness. To permit a public criterion to monitor how one looks at life, one must privately *choose* to consent to that criterion. An education which reminds youngsters that they are constantly, freely, baselessly, creatively choosing in this way is the kind of education we are in pursuit of. It is the education of private awareness and personal involvement. To paraphrase Professor Olson, who has written one of the finest expositions of Existentialism,[6] an education which *intensifies awareness*—indeed which possibly considers *intensity of awareness* as the working mode of an educational enterprise—is what an Existentialist would strive for.

Intensity of awareness is not to be thought of as a kind of abstract, general principle. It is always personal. It refers to the awareness of that private subjectivity, known publicly as Johnny Jones and at present sitting in the third row, but existing *pour soi*, for himself, in a world in which he is present as a value creator. It refers to Johnny's awareness of himself and of the necessity for him to decide how he wants to live his own life, his awareness of the need to decide which values he wants to live by. In practical terms, it refers to his awareness of his own precarious role as a baseless chooser who cannot escape choosing, and therefore creating, his own personal answer to all normative and moral questions that come up in his classroom or in his experience outside of school.

A youngster who becomes fully aware of himself as the shaper of his own life, aware of the fact that he must take charge of that life and make it his own statement of what a human being *ought* to be—this is the individual who has been brought beyond mere intellectual discipline, beyond mere subject matter, beyond mere enculturation, beyond mere "fundamental dispositions," to the exotic but supremely human zone we spoke of earlier, the zone of value creation where selves create their own selves beyond the reach of teacher and textbook.

THE EXISTENTIAL MOMENT: NOTES ON AN EXISTENTIALIST PSYCHOLOGY

But the argument, so far, is highly speculative and merely symbolic. Can this high-sounding Existential "definition" of education be translated into some kind of working theory of how boys and girls are to be approached in the environs of a school? I think it can, but by way of entree to such a theory we have need of some discussion of the psychology of subjectivity.

Somewhere in the general vicinity of puberty—whether related to this organic change or not, I am not sure—comes a moment in the subjective life of the individual which I speak of as the "Existential Moment." It is the moment when the individual first discovers himself as existing. It is the abrupt onset, the charged beginning, of awareness of the phenomenon of one's own presence in the world as a person. Prior to this point there is no such awareness. Children do not know what they are; they do not even know *that* they are. Childhood is a pre-Existential phase of human life.

Then, with a certain suddenness—perhaps in front of a mirror looking straight into one's own eyes, perhaps while walking alone in a field, perhaps in a crowded store—an unusual flicker of insight opens a new door in consciousness. "I am here. I am an 'I' in the world. I am a person." Professor Spiegelberg has reported empirically, for the first time as far as I know, on this remarkable phenomenon. In a fascinating article entitled "On the 'I-Am-Me' Experience in Childhood and Adolescence,"[7] he reveals how this inner glimpse of one's own being has first occurred in different individuals.

I don't think, however, that empirical studies are really needed. I have discussed the Existential Moment with my university classes for several years. With absolutely no empirical evidence to call on in support of the reality of this phenomenon, I have had no difficulty whatsoever in making sense to my students. They know what I am talking about. Although the Moment occurs at different times—one student reported it as early as four years of age—the preponderance of my listeners nod assent that this awareness did occur at a more or less specifiable place in their past, as it did in my own.

The visual representation of the phenomenon presented in Figure 1 may help. Here I have tried to show the Existential Moment, the onset of the self's awareness of its own existing, as dividing the life span into two radically different phases, the "pre-Existential" and the "Existential." I think the passage from the one to the

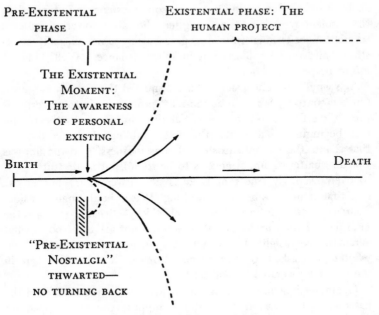

FIGURE 1. *The Existential Moment*

other of these phases is critical, and an understanding of it can help us think about education.[8]

For one thing, the transition is perhaps more profoundly turbulent than the well-advertised string of adjustments we attach to adolescence and teen-agery. There is a certain quiet agony in reaching and crossing this critical boundary. The individual sees himself for the first time as *responsible* for his own conduct. Society recognizes this boundary line in its treatment of children; children cannot be "held responsible" for what they do because they are not yet "existential," that is, self-aware subjectivities capable of *feeling* a sense of responsibility.[9] The Existential Moment is the beginning of the sense of being responsible.

It is never easy to become aware of this sense for the first time. I do not suppose there is an individual alive who cannot remember striking out at the world in some manner upon feeling the first shock wave of this explosion in the consciousness. It is typified in the insolent remark of the youngster who, after cowering under a severe tongue-lashing from his parents for some allegedly monstrous misdemeanor, blurts out in sullen defiance, "Well, I didn't *ask* to be born, ya know!"

We would make a mistake if we dismissed this remark as trivial. On the contrary, it is one of the most profound of utterances; it is the child's first complete existential thought. It marks the tremulous beginning of maturity, the first rumbling of the earthquake that shakes the self into existential consciousness. And the irony is that its shattering importance is to be found not in its truth (it *is* so overpoweringly true that there is no answer to it) but in the fact that it means absolutely nothing! We unhesitatingly consider such a remark idiotic and ridiculous. Why? Because it bears the fatal flaw of total irrelevance. "So you did not ask to be born; what a remarkable insight! But you have spoken a vacuous verity. For, whether you asked to come or not, *here you are!* Here you are in the world, answerable for yourself!"

Could we imagine building any kind of truly human life on the basis of such a vacant proposition? Suppose you are stopped for speeding on the highway. The patrolman, leaning in the car window, gives you not only a ticket with a stiff fine in prospect but a verbal "chewing out" for which policemen are famous. And suppose you answer his grim, blue sermon by saying quietly, "Yes, officer, but I didn't ask to be born." *O Lex, miserere nobis!*

The above phenomenon I have chosen to call "Pre-Existential Nostalgia." It is Everychild's desire to climb back into the womb of nonresponsibility. It is a desire we all have—to somehow regain what has sentimentally been called "the innocence of youth." Youth's innocence is not mere naïveté about worldly things; after all, there is nothing particularly attractive about being ingenuous or unknowing. No. The attraction and charm of innocence is the feeling of relief over not being personally responsible for what we are. We would love to retain all the knowledge and worldly perception of our post-Existential Moment experience if we could simply deduct that encumbrance of responsibility.

But, as we all know, it cannot be done. We have reached the point of no return. Once the Existential Moment has occurred, there is no turning back. Sherwood Anderson's phrase "the sadness of sophistication" catches this immediate, post-Moment mood. We discover ourselves as having "turned up" in the world, being here, inescapably answerable for the meaning and quality of one human life. It is a big order, like the heart-stopping experience of being served a summons, a summons to do something with that life *deserving* the predicate "human." It should not surprise anyone if this awakening sets in motion certain traumas of the spirit, such as aching nostalgia, sadness.

But what lies *beyond* the initial reactions is more important. After these immediate sensations have passed there can issue a feeling of great power and thrust. For the first time, I am in a position to see my life as my own. I am in charge of everything that happens from that Existential Moment forward. The world that opens out to me, after this remarkable event, is baffling and difficult. Tillich speaks of it as essentially an "encounter with meaninglessness." But it is important for us as adults and for youngsters in school to remember that a world of meaninglessness, a world without meaning already woven into and embedded in it, is a world which, in a manner of speaking, is "on our side." That is, it presents possibilities without exacting the reciprocal tribute of human compliance. If there is no a priori meaning to it—and this obviously is how the Existentialist sees it—then we as free subjectivities can creatively assign meaning to it.

Why is it that "meaninglessness" is so generally thought to be an epithet, a philosophical swear word, a term of scorn and rebuke? The Existentialist can tell you: It is because men still want to "escape from freedom"; they still exhibit a "failure of nerve," as William James used to say. Even the Experimentalists feel ill at ease in the company of the word "meaninglessness." But why should they? A world without meaning already contained in it is the only kind of world where human freedom really makes any ultimate sense. A world *with* meaning is a world where compliances are owed, where certain understandings are legitimate and therefore expected, a world to which man's relation must be, in some degree, *unfree*.[10]

The world of the Existentialist is void of all prior meaning. It is a world in which meanings are human inventions and creations. It is therefore a world that is really *open*, in the most thoroughgoing interpretation of this word. It spreads out before us in a luminous, wondrous way. And it is this kind of world to which the Existentialist would hope to introduce the young. It is in this kind of genuinely meaningless existence that the free human project can get started, the project of *creating* meanings and fashioning an essence of man as it might be made incarnate in one, real, actual, historical person.

If the world offers all but requires nothing—if it is really *open* and man is *free*—then the human project to which the young are to be invited is the project of shaping something unique and singular completely on their own, a human life to which they can refer by saying, "Here. This is my contribution to the developing essence of man. This, my life as I see how it might be lived, is my 'vote' on what man means in the world." It is really a creative task, the literal creation of a somethingness out of a meaningless nothingness, a "sculpturing of one's figure in the world," as Sartre puts it. An education which grips a child by his moral coat collars and lifts him up to see over the crowd to the task of taking *personal responsibility* for being human—that education can be called Existentialist.

THE EDUCATIONAL TASK

Specifically what kind of education would it be? The significance of the Existential Moment is that it occurs at approximately the halfway mark of the conventional twelve-year educational career of the youngster in the United States. I should judge that for most young people the Moment strikes in the late elementary or junior high school years.[11] Thus when Existentialists speak of an educational theory, they will refer to a theory having its orientation and focus primarily upon the secondary phases of learning. Elementary education, in all likelihood, could assume a variety of forms and still be adequate to an Existential secondary education; the lower grades necessarily deal with the individual before he is existentially awake. Existentialism, as an educational philosophy, can therefore afford to be officially indifferent to and disinterested toward elementary educational theory.

In its most general terms, the task of education can be stipulated somewhat as follows: to provide the occasions and circumstances for the awakening and intensification of awareness. To be more specific and concrete, education must become an act of *discovery*. But the question is, discovery of what? If the Brunerian psychologists can speak of "discovery" of the structure of subject matter, let the Existentialists be permitted a substitute prepositional object:

Let education be *the discovery of responsibility!* Let learning be the sharp and vivid awakening of the learner to the sense of being personally answerable for his own life. But, lest we turn such a phrase into a mere slogan, we must remember that

> . . . this responsibility is of a very particular type. . . . I am responsible for everything, in fact, except for my very responsibility, for I am not the foundation of my being. Therefore everything takes place as if I were compelled to be responsible. I am abandoned in the world, not in the sense that I might remain abandoned and passive in a hostile universe like a board floating on the water, but rather in the sense that I find myself suddenly alone and without help, engaged in a world for which I bear the whole responsibility without being able, whatever I do, to tear myself away from this responsibility for an instant. For I am responsible for my very desire of fleeing responsibilities.[12]

Let education be the process by which we awaken in each learner the truth that *he is responsible for his very desire to flee responsibility;* ". . . the peculiar character of human-reality is that it is without excuse."[13] Can we drive this nail straight into the very center of each awakening subjectivity who comes to school?

A world with no excuses! What an exhilarating possibility. A world the Existentialist dreams of as genuinely worthy of lasting educational effort.

INVOLVEMENT AND THE AFFECTIVE MODE

Any program of instruction which sets out on this precarious journey will navigate by the proposition that the child must somehow learn to *feel* his freedom and responsibility in the most personal terms. It is expected, therefore, that such an educational program will give greater than usual prominence to educational experiences in which *personal involvement* is magnified and intensified.

In a manner of speaking, the Experimentalists and Progressives have carried us a good way down this road. They have involved the youngster much more than is customary in the learning process itself. But they have finally yielded, as indicated earlier, to the siren song of the social psychologists, who insist that involvement must be understood as a relation between the individual and the *group;* involvement is always thought to mean some characteristic of experience which concerns *others* and which can be referred to by such terms as "group dynamics," "human relations," "sociograms," and "peer influence." It is by now a truism that behavioral scientists almost never speak of involvement as personal, emotional, or privately *affective* in nature, because *such involvement does not lend itself to the conventional forms of empirical inquiry.*

To the Existentialist, therefore, Experimentalist and Progressive theory in education can be put down as essentially bloodless and emotion-free. It is a kind of detached, "cool cat" way of dealing with human experience. "Low-conflict" rapport with others—in neighborhood or classroom—is the unarguable first principle. A passionless acceptance of the *method* by which disputes are resolved and by which the whole dialectic of social existence is managed therefore takes over as the primary obligation of the youngster in school. The canons of *inquiry,* in all the splendid ramifications of that favorite word of the scientific mind, now become the prime aim of instruction.

This is what the Experimentalist really means by his pedagogy of "problem solving." It is a pedagogy dedicated to the "training of intelligence" in the management of life's problematic situations. But, while the situations may be problematic, the method by which they are to be managed is not. It is sure. Hence, Experimentalist education really means winning the student over to an acceptance of this method, "precertified" and endorsed by a scientific civilization, by which all experience can be organized and to which all of life's difficulties are referable.

"Involvement," looked at in this superficial way, eventually takes back all that it promises to give. It simply substitutes a new pedagogical imperium for an old one. It provides the child with a *cer-*

tain method instead of a *certain* truth. "Certainty" has not been dislodged as the ultimate educational principle; it is still very much in place. Indeed, the "quest for certainty"—in method and technique—continues as feverish as ever.

How are we going to get over this persistent, chronic nostalgia for certainty? One way is to understand "involvement" in a different and deeper way. To the Existentialist, involvement means the experience of getting personally implicated in the situations of life. In education, it means the learner's experience of getting personally implicated in his subject matter and in the situation around him. It means being aroused by questions of bad and good, right and wrong, pro and con, yes and no. In short, it means awakening to the normative quality of experience—in a book, in a teacher's remark, in a classroom situation.

Contemporary education, whether traditional or progressive, is well known for its failure to implicate the child in moral and ethical questions. Such questions are allegedly too touchy or too personal for classroom discussion. The American parent is notoriously jumpy about having his child discuss questions of premarital sexual intercourse, the divinity of the Virgin Mary, the admission of Red China to the United Nations. And this is just the Existentialist's point. By insulating the learner from thinking about and *feeling* the intensity of explosive questions, the parent and the parent-intimidated teacher cannot possibly awaken a youngster to his existential freedom and to his sense of individual responsibility for directing his own moral life. The child remains passive and "cool" about the struggle between right and wrong in the world. Teaching continues to be carried on in the third person; the phenomena to which the learner's attention is directed are all outside his own skin. The subject matters of today's schools are really "object" matters. They deal with the world beyond the schoolhouse door, seldom with the child's own response to what is going on. The learner does not see the possibility for asserting a personal, subjective view on anything. He is given the impression that asserting such a view is somehow naughty and uncouth.

Experimentalism as an educational philosophy is just as guilty on this score as any other. It is, qua educational philosophy, just as devoted to third-person teaching as those theories it purports to supplant. In Progressivist schools, the "method" (the project method, the scientific method, the method of inquiry) rather than some preexistent "truth" now serves as the third-person "it" which the learner is expected to learn and to which he is expected to orient his life.

THE EPISTEMOLOGY OF APPROPRIATION

We may now extrapolate from all of this the first working hypothesis of the Existentialist philosopher of education: Whatever it is that boys and girls are expected to acquire in school must somehow be looked at from the first-person vantage.

We have in the verb "appropriate" a possible access route to this first-person mode. Etymologically, the word means "to make one's own." We are too likely, in a materialist, capitalist civilization, to misunderstand this term as belonging only to transactions of physical property; to appropriate something in an economic sense is obviously to deprive someone else of appropriating it. But in the epistemological sense the word can take on other connotations. It can mean simply the personal taking and adopting of something that is available to all. What is taken—ideas, attitudes, points of view—is common property. What is uncommon and really unique is how each of us uses and appropriates these "data" in interpreting the world.

One might say that a whole new understanding of the word "truth" is going to be called for, an understanding whereby the learner's *feeling toward* truth comes to play as significant a role as his mere cognitive understanding of it. In a passage concerning the ontological underpinnings of Existentialist epistemology Ralph Harper puts it this way:

> . . . it is possible to say that there is a world and there is truth; but it is not possible to say that the world is only this or that and truth this or that. Man's relation to truth, whatever some men say, is a leaning toward, a stretching out at, a longing for that which is present but not fully, clearly named.[14]

> . . . neither the world nor truth has a label on it, telling what

*it is and how it is related to the other. There is no way but the
way of individual judgment.*[15]

Knowledge is always in part subjective. That is, for anything to
be true, it must first pass into and be taken hold of by some subjective consciousness. It must be *chosen*, i.e., appropriated, before
it can be true for that consciousness. Knowledge is not something
purely objective and laid out to be learned (as the traditional educator might say), nor is it something merely functional and useful
in the management of experience (as the Experimentalist might
say). At bottom, knowledge *becomes* knowledge only when a subjectivity takes hold of it and puts it into his own life. In this sense,
then, the individual may be said to be responsible for his own
knowledge.[16]

What could such a statement mean? Let us take the case of
history. Here is a body of knowledge, a subject matter which appears to be outside of both teacher and learner. It lays claim in our
common sense to being purely objective truth: "X occurred. What's
done is done. The fact that X occurred is a hard, brute, objective
fact." Now, is the Existentialist about to assert that the individual
is responsible for X's having occurred? Of course not. What the
Existentialist asserts is that the individual is responsible for at-
taching *meaning* to the fact that X occurred; he is responsible
for endowing that cold, brute fact with human significance. It is
in this sense that the individual creates meanings and, in the creating, appropriates "X occurred" as an article of subject matter.

Can the youngster in school do this? Why not? Every school
child studies the American Revolution. By general consent, it is
one of the big X's in our past. But what does it mean? This, to the
Existentialist, is always an open question, to be decided by each
individual. Each student must become the "baseless chooser" at
this point. He must create and therefore become personally responsible for the meaning of the American Revolution for *his own life*.
And if you ask why he *must*, the answer is that he cannot avoid
taking some kind of attitude toward that historical X once he cog-
nitively understands it; he is compelled by his existential freedom
to hold a point of view regarding it. Even if he is indifferent to it
or quickly forgets all about it, that is his point of view, his created

meaning vis-à-vis the American Revolution. In that episode he has brought a meaning into existence.

> . . . human history would have to be finished before a particular event . . . could receive a definitive meaning. [What is the meaning of the American Revolution?] He who would like to decide the question today forgets that the historian [or the history teacher] is himself historical; that is, that he historicizes himself by illuminating "history" in the light of his projects and of those of his society. Thus it is necessary to say that the meaning of the social past is always "in suspense."[17]

If the above is true of "social history," it is equally true of one's own personal history. I make the meanings of my own past:

> . . . the meaning of the past is strictly dependent on my present project. This certainly does not mean that I can make the meaning of my previous acts vary in any way I please; quite the contrary, it means that the fundamental project which I am decides absolutely the meaning which [my] past . . . can have for me. . . . I alone in fact can decide at each moment the bearing of the past. . . . by projecting myself toward my ends, I preserve the past with me, and by action I decide its meaning. . . . Thus all my past is there pressing, urgent, imperious, but its meanings and the orders which it gives me I choose by the very project of my end.[18]

It was noted toward the close of Chapter 3 that we each create our own limits by the goals we set for ourselves. We saw that the youngster who is weak in mathematics finds this weakness a hindrance to him by virtue of his desire to become an engineer. His *choice* of career *creates* the hindrance. The same phenomenon occurs in the appropriation of historical subject matter, social or personal. The meanings to be attached to the past are created by each of us in light of our own personal life projects. Events in the past take on significance, they come to bear on our lives, only by virtue of our individually having first decided to live in a certain way or on behalf of certain values. Only when this primary choice has been made does history shape up as being meaningful or meaningless. In this sense, then, I create my own history. And my act of creation, the *creation of meanings*, is referred to by the Existentialist as "appropriation."

THE CURRICULUM OF A FREE EXISTENT

What we have said with this lengthy example of history can now be generalized to refer to every subject matter in the school. Cognitive understanding of mathematics, of biology, of government and literature and geography and all the rest—of course. But let us attend to the student's *attitude* toward these boxes of knowledge, his leaning toward, his stretching out to these granite blocks of truth. This is where Existential education begins.

The existentialist attitude toward knowledge radically affects the teaching of those subjects which are dependent upon systems of thought or frames of reference: it states that school subjects are only tools for the realization of subjectivity.[19]

This view of the curriculum is a specialized version of the Existentialist's entire epistemology. It is an epistemology diametrically opposed to the so-called "Spectator Theory" of knowledge made popular by the Realists. It is the view of knowledge not from the standpoint of the spectator but from the standpoint of the *actor*, onstage and actively implicated in the "role" of man.

Look at knowledge, if you will, in the most traditional way of the Spectator Theorist, viz., as encyclopedic in character. Knowledge may be thought of as an organized universe of cognitive propositions such as might be found in the Britannica. Every library is a kind of "walk-in" encyclopedia, a storage vault of information. But note, he who walks in is the center of the action; he must decide which propositions, among the world's billions of propositions, are meaningful and significant and therefore worth believing. He is the actor, the active agent. He chooses his knowledge.

An allegorical aside may clarify this last. It is as if man had been cast in a role for which no part had been written. We have awakened to our existence to discover a script in our hands. But the script is blank. We "write" our own script in speaking hitherto unwritten lines; we act it out, ad libs and all. Indeed, the whole play, all of life, is ad lib.

Part of the dialogue we invent and act out, i.e., part of our stream of ad libs, is epistemological; that is, some of the lines we speak are propositions of a cognitive sort. We utter possible truths about the world. But they are all uttered from the standpoint of the *actor* who sees them as true only in light of the role he is trying to develop by pronouncing them. If, therefore, some of the dialogue is scientific, it is because those who speak these lines are "playing the role" of man—"creating the part," as they say in the theater—as if they intended man's meaning in the world to be "the vehicle of scientific cognition."

But there are other lines, other ad libs, other soliloquies, other asides that can be spoken. Those who speak them have a different idea of how the "part" of man should be played. There is no preterhuman playwright who has certified one set of lines or one "interpretation" of the role as more authentic than any other. Each of us creates his own interpretation of the part.

Working from this allegory, we may say that the library of any university or the curriculum of any school, insofar as it represents the extant knowledge of the world, represents the "scripts" that have thus far been written, the lines spoken by others in their interpretation of the "role" of man. They are there for the taking, but each learner must do the taking. They are possible lines to be spoken if the learner wishes to employ them in realizing his own subjectivity. The curriculum is not there to be mastered (as the traditionalist would say), nor is it there to be experienced (as the Experimentalist might say). It is there to be *chosen*. The subject matters and experiences in a curriculum shall be merely *available*; to be learned, they must first be opted for, sought out, and appropriated by the student.[20]

One might well ask at this point whether, in all that is presently "available" in contemporary conventional curricula, any subjects or learning experiences would particularly lend themselves to Existentialist development. Are there components of today's curricula which might be adaptable to the above analysis, which seem to provide even in their present form the possibility of teaching in the first-person mode wherein genuine, individualized appropriation can be encouraged? Certainly whatever experiences in the school are most likely to arouse the individual's own private way of looking at life will be elevated to first position in anything that might some day be called an Existentialist school. Are there such experiences in present-day school programs?

I think there are two possibilities for an affirmative answer to this question. By far the more obvious but, in the long run, perhaps of lesser significance is that region of the curriculum we customarily label the *arts*. Experiences in music, the dance, drama, creative writing, painting, and the plastic arts seem to me the chief contenders for this kind of education. In these "subjects," if you want to call them that, the idea has already gained headway that what the child produces in his classroom or homework assignments is very largely *his*. (If this is not altogether true of music, I think it is still true of the other areas mentioned.) We can credit the Progressive educator for this development; he is the one who, in these areas, liberated the child from the heavy hand both of traditional canons of form and of contemporary, "other-directed" conventions of style. The learner's dance or short story, his snatch of dialogue or role playing, his clay figure or water color is somehow *not* expected to match what has gone before. It is expected to be his own authentic expression of what he sees in his own world. Not only that, but the motivation to produce these "works" is not primarily to exhibit them to others but rather to work out, from the center of one's private experience, certain meanings that the world may have for oneself.

If Existentialism ever gains a foothold in educational thinking in this country, it will probably begin its work in these "self-creating" subject matters. Thanks to the Progressive, we have already established a precedent to work from, a precedent for the kind of teaching in which the learner sees himself in the role of creative innovator in the learning process.

The less obvious but eventually more significant area of learning is, unfortunately, one that has no name. We shall call it "normative." Included in this category are not only subject matters per se but experiences of all sorts which awaken the decision-making awarenesses of the learner.

Among the subject matters of a normative sort, I believe that history and literature would probably provide the most fuel for an Existentialist teacher. As indicated in the previous example of history, the implicit question of *meaning* and *significance* always lies just beneath the surface of historical subject matter. The question "So what?" can be made explicit on an instant's notice in every history classroom during the study of virtually any historical period or any particular event. If the old cliché that the purpose of studying history is to illuminate the present has any meaning, it must be that the "illumination" is of a normative sort; that is, such study presents to us various hypotheses as to how life in the present might be lived, how we might solve our problems. The whole point of examining the past is to identify really live options on the management of present events in the name of a desired future. If we are to "learn from history," what else could the cliché possibly mean?

Every historiographer grants that the past does not give us direct instructions on how to manage the present. It merely helps us, as he might put it, to *understand* the present. But of what worth would mere understanding be if it did not at least suggest what was possible in the way of social action? Such aloof, insulated "understanding" would be a splendid luxury, but it could hardly persuade anybody to labor at the study of history. It would be a case of "present-ism" in its most vicious form, having no critical dimension concerning what was right and what was wrong about contemporary civilization. History can be understood only forward, not backward. "It is the future which decides whether the past is living or dead."[21] For the past to live, it must in one way or another awaken possibilities for things to come, the region out ahead where human projects are worked out.

The study of literature is equally relevant for the awakening of strategic choice making on the part of the learner. And by "strategic" I mean choice making of a magnitude which bears on the shape and direction of an entire human life. Shakespeare's *Hamlet*, a perennial figure, comes immediately to mind. It is a work in which the agonies of personal definition make a persistent whisper to the student: "What would *you* have done?" Wherever ethical questions are raised for which convenient precedents in present-day experience are not available—there one will find the kinds of literature capable of arousing the existential awareness of the learner.

A literature of even greater power, in my judgment, is twentieth-century drama. We have grown weary of Hollywood happy endings; modern playwrights have helped us rediscover the "tragic sense of life." Tragedy is not merely the blatantly *un*happy ending, or the melodramatic, but that struggle to make sense of human existence and to find personal meaning in an apparently indifferent world. In this kind of struggle genuine affective involvement can be generated. In the student's personal involvement with the works of such authors, let us say, as Samuel Beckett, Tennessee Williams, Arthur Miller, Jean Paul Sartre, or Albert Camus may be found the makings of an "awakening" experience for him.

For the less literary student, the nuclear-age novel can awaken some of the same feelings. Nevil Shute's *On the Beach* and Eugene Burdick and Harvey Wheeler's *Fail-Safe* are the sort of semifiction that raises the ultimate existential question: If the human race were to be burned to cinders, what would be the world's loss? It is this kind of question that every human being must sooner or later confront. It is a question which somehow stands at the gate of authenticity. Until the secondary school student is willing to ponder it and attempt his own answer—without directives from priest, or parent, or teacher—he cannot claim that he has really grown up.

A few pages back I remarked that the "normative" segment of the curriculum must include not only subject matters but experiences of all kinds in which the sharp, pro-and-con ethical dimension is intensified. Unfortunately, concrete illustrations of such experiences are scarce. Both traditional and modern schools are notoriously antiseptic when it comes to admitting such "foreign elements" into the school's program. In the traditional school, there is thought to be some set of *principles* by which all ethical questions can be settled. In modern schools, an impersonal *method* clears up moral indecision. In either case, the individual's personal awareness of having to choose his own answers is blunted and made numb. Carl Jung once made a similar observation:

> As a rule the individual is so unconscious that he altogether fails to see his own potentialities for decision. Instead he is constantly

and anxiously looking around for external rules and regulations which can guide him in his perplexity. Aside from general human inadequacy, a good deal of the blame for this rests with education, which promulgates the old generalizations and says' nothing about the secrets of private experience. Every effort is made to teach idealistic beliefs or conduct which people know in their hearts they can never live up to, and such ideals are preached by officials who know that they themselves have never lived up to these high standards and never will. What is more, nobody ever questions the value of this kind of teaching.[22]

Well, Existentialism *does* question this kind of teaching, and vigorously. It questions all teaching in the ethical sphere which depersonalizes the ethical act of *deciding*. And, as I have previously suggested, it seems to me that the Experimentalist's "examine-the-public-consequences" ethic and the Progressive educator's "project-method-of-inquiry" way of educating in moral judgment are both just as numbingly *de*personal as any theistic decalogue or any metaphysical imperative of an earlier philosophic tradition. They deliberately play down private, individual decision-making in favor of social determinants. They intentionally make of the school an arena in which the group mind is shown to be superior to the individual mind. All the apparatus of Progressive educational theory— group process, social promotion, the "whole-child" concept, the project method, sociograms, sociodrama, human relations (the list is long)—has been installed in our schools because of our abiding belief that the *group* thinking, the *group* considering, the *group* choosing is a more authentic and reliable avenue to true humanity than the *individual* thinking, considering, and choosing.

Moral judgment and personal character, if no one bridles at the use of this old-fashioned term, have their origin in the subjective self. This is where ethical education belongs.

. . . the individual who wishes to have an answer to the problem of evil as it is posed today has need, first and foremost, of self-knowledge—that is, the utmost possible knowledge of his own wholeness. He must know relentlessly how much good he can do and what crimes he is capable of, and must beware of regarding the one as real and the other as illusion. Both are elements within *his nature, and both are bound to come to light in him, should he wish—as he ought—to live without self-deception or self-delusion.*[23]

THE "EXTRACURRICULAR" MODE
OF DISCOVERY

If the curriculum of the Existentialist school is intended to be merely available, to be there for the asking, the choosing, the appropriating, then it is obvious that the development of so-called "extracurricular activities" in the American school may bear some analysis. As we all know, boys and girls frequently find in these activities the kind of self-creating experiences that the regular curriculum does not offer. Here is appropriation in almost its literal sense, the sense of making an experience "one's own."

It comes as something of a surprise to find youngsters in these activities actually returning to the rigorous difficulties of the curriculum itself which they allegedly seek to escape: Chess clubs demand a concentration in logic far beyond any course in algebra or geometry; school newspapers require a discipline of reportorial accuracy and of meeting deadlines even stricter than that in English; foreign language clubs enforce a "No English" rule during their sessions more insistent than any instructor's; and interscholastic athletics exact far greater agility, coordination, and sheer strength than are ever found in a course in physical education. Yet students still seek out these experiences, appropriating them in behalf of their own developing subjectivities.

Why? Under Existentialist analysis, the answer may be said to lie in a deceptively subtle psychological distinction between what Sartre calls the attitude of "seriousness" and the attitude of "play." The "serious" attitude may be characterized as that which sees man as an object, among other objects, in a world made up exclusively of objects. It is the conventional stance of all those ontologies which begin, as noted in Chapter 1, by understanding the world first and then finding man's place in it. Man, in the serious mode, is always a *consequence* of an antecedent reality; he is to be understood only in terms of an environment or temporality not of his own making, a world which is somehow more real than he is.

"The serious attitude involves starting from the world and attributing more reality to the world than to oneself; at the very least the serious man confers reality on himself to the degree to which he belongs to the world."[24]

With the assistance of this definition, we may now classify all conventional epistemologies such as Thomism, Idealism, Realism, and Experimentalism as essentially "serious." They see knowledge as man's "catalog of meanings" of a world not of his own creation. In all of these epistemologies the world is thought to contain meanings, which man, in one way or another, mines out of it. We include Experimentalism in the list because Science is the most "serious" of all epistemologies. It turns everything, including man himself, into an *object* of inquiry. As an epistemology, Science can study the world no other way. The element of human subjectivity is, by definition, incompatible with Science. The scientific attitude is therefore the finest and most thoroughgoing expression of "seriousness" in our world today.

Now, the curriculum of the typical school is the "serious" content of the world made available to the young. Because it is "serious" it always outranks the student in importance. The Existentialist educator is understandably guarded on the role of "serious" knowledge, i.e., the conventional curriculum, in the educative process. That is why he has altered the conception of the learning process from mastering or experiencing the curriculum to choosing and appropriating the curriculum. In the former convention of mastering or experiencing, the student is given the impression that he is taking on a cargo that the world somehow requires, whereas in the latter mode of choosing or appropriating what he learns, the student is given to see that he is taking on a cargo which only he himself requires, and thus he is responsible for having taken it on. In this way "serious" knowledge is rendered harmless; its "serious" quality is neutralized and disarmed by putting the choice of learning it up to the learner himself.

But when we come to the extracurriculum, we find a set of learning experiences that do not stand in need of being neutralized. They are already undertaken in an attitude quite different from that of "the serious." They are, technically speaking, "play." That is, they are undertaken only on the individual's own terms, not on terms which have been set in advance. The student outranks the activity in importance.

Play, like Kierkegaard's irony, releases subjectivity. What is play indeed if not an activity of which man is the first origin, for which man himself sets the rules, and which has no consequences except according to the rules posited.[25]

If we understand the word "play" in this technical sense, then we have in Sartre's comment perhaps the most succinct and astringent definition of extracurricular activities ever to appear in the educational literature. This, we finally see, is the secret of such activities, why they startle us with their power to quicken growth in the young. They "release subjectivity," they are entered into only with the understanding of the learner that *he*, not the teacher or the school or society or the logic of "seriousness," sets the rules.

If we could imagine a school in which all learning activities were pursued in a mode and attitude similar to that of present-day extracurricular programs, I think we would find ourselves in the presence of an Existentialist design for education. With the gradual increase in this aspect of the American school's work, we may be witnessing the first stages of an Existentialist educational revolution. From the feverish enthusiasm that youngsters often exhibit in throwing themselves into these unrequired experiences, we may conclude that the young have arrived at an appreciation of this kind of learning far in advance of routine-ridden teachers and administrators; educational officialdom is inclined to give only grudging approval and sanction to this kind of education, in spite of the fact that, all too frequently, students are actually learning and growing more in these exercises than in the "serious" projects of a school's curriculum.

All of which means that the Existentialist school of the future may turn out to be the creation of the learners more than of those who teach. Just how such a situation might come about can be understood in the analysis of an Existentialist pedagogy, to which we turn in Chapter 6.

NOTES

1. I used to talk this way myself. See "Existentialism and Education," *Educational Theory*, Vol. IV, No. 4 (October, 1954), pp. 247–258. However, I have changed my mind about this.

2. Erich Fromm, *Escape from Freedom* (New York: Holt, Rinehart and Winston, 1941).

3. F. L. Whitmarsh, Jr., "An Inquiry into the Implications of Existentialism on Political Theory" (B.A. thesis, Harvard College, 1948), p. 7.

4. Clifton Hall, "Traditional Education," in *Ways of Looking at Educational Purpose*, Council for Basic Education, Bulletin No. 5 (January, 1961), pp. 6–11.

5. John Dewey, *Democracy and Education* (New York: The Macmillan Company, 1916), p. 383, italics in original.

6. Robert G. Olson, *An Introduction to Existentialism* (New York: Dover Publications, 1962); see especially pp. 17 and 18.

7. Herbert Spiegelberg, "On the 'I-Am-Me' Experience in Childhood and Adolescence," *Psychologia—An International Journal of Psychology in the Orient*, Vol. IV, No. 3 (September, 1961), pp. 135–146.

8. It can also help us think about psychiatry. Traditional, Freudian psychiatry was built on the principle that pre-Existential events in childhood, buried in the subconscious, can be brought forward in analysis by being actively remembered and, hence, known and understood by the patient. In this primitive Freudian theory, the patient viewed his neurosis merely as a phenomenon having its origin in the past. Once having understood the alleged "cause" of his neurosis, he would symbolically say to himself, "So *that's* why I'm neurotic. . .," and would not do anything about it, since the past is in principle out of reach. See Jean-Paul Sartre, *Being and Nothingness*, trans., by Hazel E. Barnes (New York: Philosophical Library, 1956), p. 458.

Existential psychiatry (and other contemporary theories) reject this principle insisting that therapy lies in pointing the patient's attention to the future and awakening his awareness of the fact that, once having comprehended the character of his neurotic behavior, he is from that moment on a free chooser of his conduct and no longer has any excuse for being neurotic. The impact of modern psychiatry is, therefore, to arouse and awaken to its fullest intensity the patient's sense of present and future responsibility for the character of his life. See Rollo May et al., *Existence, A New Dimension in Psychiatry and Psychology* (New York: Basic Books, Inc., 1958).

9. We should note in passing that the psychology of criminology recognizes it also. The plea of "temporary insanity" is now defined in criminal cases as the temporary absence of the sense of responsibility.

10. The Experimentalist is sure to object to this characterization, claiming that his "world," like that of the Existentialist, does not have a priori meanings written into it. That is correct, except for one, namely, the idea that tentative, functional, "group" meaning is possible, and that there is a method, Science, by which this meaning can be mined out of experience. The one a priori meaning the Experimentalists permit themselves can therefore be stated somewhat as follows: "The world can be understood, even if only in an operational, situation-by-situation manner. What we are reasonably sure of is that the method is secure; this method does indeed yield reliable meanings." This is the Experimentalist's quiet, unobtrusive "escape from freedom." It is, ironically, his clandestine "failure of nerve." He cannot stand living in a genuinely meaningless world.

11. Professor Spiegelberg believes the age of incidence is somewhat lower, i.e., the age of eight of nine, or in second or third grade.

12. Sartre, op. cit., pp. 555–556.

13. Ibid., p. 555.

14. Ralph Harper, "Significance of Existence and Recognition for Education," chap. VII in N. B. Henry, ed., Modern Philosophies and Education, 54th Yearbook of the National Society for the Study of Education, Part I (Chicago: Published by the Society, 1955), p. 233.

15. Ibid., p. 232.

16. See George F. Kneller, Existentialism and Education (New York: Philosophical Library, 1958), p. 59.

17. Sartre, op. cit., p. 501.

18. Ibid., p. 498.

19. Kneller, op. cit., p. 63.

20. See a description of such a school, Summerhill, in Chapter 6.

21. Sartre, op. cit., p. 499.

22. "Jung's View of Christianity," recorded and edited by Aniela Jaffe, The Atlantic Monthly, Vol. 211, No. 1 (January, 1963), p. 62.

23. Ibid.

24. Sartre, op. cit., p. 580.

25. Ibid.

6

AN EXISTENTIALIST

PEDAGOGY

It must be clear by now that Existentialism is not a philosophy in the conventional sense. It is not a body of thought about the nature of world and man. Its message is far simpler and at the same time more profound, viz., Existentialism wishes merely to establish the starting place for the philosophical enterprise itself, the place from which all thought about the meaning of life must set out. This place is the human *self*.

Existential education assumes the responsibility of awakening each individual to the full intensity of his own selfhood.

An instructional method which pretends pursuit of such a goal must obviously possess some working knowledge of the "self." Just what is it? Certainly, the "self" is not an object in the world with a static essence or whatness. Nor is the "self" merely a verbal construct to stand for an occurrence or event in an empirical sociology. The word "self" must be understood as a phenomenon—literally, from the Greek, "that which reveals itself"—best represented, as the earlier chapters have indicated, by the word *awareness*." The technical Existentialist "definition" (if there is a definition) of "self," therefore, might be "the phenomenon of the awareness of subjectivity"—that is, the awareness of being an unanalyzable, undefinable point of origin for all subsequent awarenesses. It is this prime awareness of self which becomes possible, but not automatic, on the occasion of the Existential Moment. And it is this awareness which the Existentialist teacher would seek to intensify.

As the earlier chapters have shown, there are three constituent awarenesses which make up the psychological content of "self":

1. I am a *choosing* agent, unable to avoid choosing my way through life.
2. I am a *free* agent, absolutely free to set the goals of my own life.
3. I am a *responsible* agent, personally accountable for my free choices as they are revealed in how I live my life.

The teacher's imperative is to arrange the learning situation in such a way as to bring home the truth of these three propositions to every individual.

THE SOCRATIC PARADIGM

It is something of a pleasant surprise to find in the educational theory of antiquity a paradigm to work from, namely, the classic figure of Socrates as teacher. Unfortunately, however, the paradigm is ambiguous.

For one thing, Socrates' injunction "Know thyself" bears a superficial and misleading resemblance to the Existentialist injunction for each person to become aware of his own subjectivity. Socrates, and the Greeks generally, viewed the self as some sort of essential content in the human structure; if an individual could be summoned to "Know thyself," supposedly the self was an entity that could be known. There is nothing in Existentialism to coincide with this understanding. Indeed, the self as a transcending phenomenon fashioned out of free choices is supremely *un*known and *un*knowable. One can become aware of the self as a phenomenon, but not know it.

Another ambiguity lies in the fact that Socrates' famous interrogative method took two forms. On some occasions Socrates posed questions whose answers he already knew; on other occasions, he posed questions whose answers he did *not* know but was earnestly seeking. The former instances are represented in those episodes in Plato's dialogues where we most often meet him in the teacher's role. The classic illustration is to be found in *The Meno*, wherein Socrates proceeds, through an artful line of questioning, to get an ignorant slave boy to formulate the Pythagorean theorem. In this pedagogic exercise, Socrates knew in advance the conclusion toward which his teaching was directed. Every question therefore enjoyed an a priori focus and intent. What appeared on the surface to be a kind of "psychic remembering" on the part of the pupil led Socrates' student Plato to formulate his notion of learning as reminiscence or recollection of a previously known set of ideas. In reality, however, most of the "remembering" was already built into the structure of the questions by virtue of the planned sequence of queries. In a very real sense, modern programmed instruction had its origin in this now famous episode in *The Meno*, in the ordered, sequential arrangement of the questions by which one understanding, and then another, and then another could be elicited step by step from the individual. Indeed, Socrates in this mode is sometimes alluded to as the father of all programmed learning.

The latter instances of questioning represented Socrates' other methodological mode: to seek for truth which he did *not* already possess. He ambled about Athens asking questions, some of them extremely embarrassing to the alleged wise men of the day and to the people in power. (As we all know, his incessant questions made him appear to his infuriated fellow citizens as a nuisance and troublemaker and they finally sentenced him to the cup of hemlock.) The bulk of Plato's dialogues show him in these kinds of interchanges. In *The Republic* and *The Theaetetus*, for example, Socrates is genuinely seeking after that which he does *not* understand and does *not* know; he is the epitome of the *seeker after truth*. The irony, however, is that we do not picture Socrates in these episodes as a teacher. He seems to us more like the inquirer or what we would now call the researcher. He is probing for new truth, and we do not customarily associate this activity with the direct act of teaching.[1] But here is precisely where Socrates foreshadows the Existentialist's educational theory. We must renew and reactivate this association of the teacher with the inquirer. We must revive the Socratic paradigm, not in the mode of *The Meno* but in the mode of *The Republic*. And I do not mean that the Existentialist teacher is always searching for new truth in the manner of the "serious" research scholar. Rather, he is searching for personal truth. Personal truth is always *new* to the individual searching for it himself; and, for that matter, it is always new to the teacher also.

Thus, if we adopt the Socratic paradigm, the teacher will concentrate on asking those questions to which he does *not* know the answer. In the most literal and profound of ways, he will learn along with his students.

The understanding of teaching as the asking of questions to which no one knows the answer will no doubt seem outrageously bizarre. It certainly runs counter to all conventional conceptions of teaching and learning. Moreover, it places the teacher under heavy obligations of imagination and insight. It is not easy to ask such questions; anyone who has attempted the "Socratic method" knows that it is one of the most difficult of teaching procedures. But difficulty must be measured against yield, namely, the possible awakening of the student to his awareness of choice, freedom, and responsibility in his own selfhood.

SOME EXAMPLES

The arts

We saw in the previous chapter that the arts represent one portion of conventional curricula that would possibly be susceptible to Existentialist treatment. We have at last outgrown the "copying" phase and the "representational" phase of art instruction. We have graduated to a newer methodological position which places the teacher in the role of "evoker" and "awakener" of the child's artistic expression. Noticeably absent from art classrooms is the insistence upon following the canons of some alleged artistic standard. In its place is the insistence by the teacher that the student stand on his own and by himself in portraying the world in water color, in oil, in soap or clay, as *he* sees it and *not* as his teacher or his classmates or the so-called "masters" see it. The teacher is, I think, enacting the Socratic paradigm by arousing the pupil to artistic expression which the teacher cannot anticipate. The teacher does not know in advance what he is after; all he knows is that it is important for the pupil to *feel* his own experience through the medium of his paintbrush or carving knife or cutting tool. *What* the student creates is less important than that he *does* create something which he can see as his own private artistic statement about his experience.

For students who may be ill at ease in the manual arts, the teacher may employ experiences in the literary arts of short-story writing and poetic expression. Spontaneity is the principal caution; nothing is quite so preposterous as to "assign" a student the task of writing an original poem "to be handed in tomorrow." But, wherever poetic or prose inclinations reveal themselves, the teacher should immediately seize on such opportunities and quicken the student's desire to express himself in his own way. In this connection, I am reminded of the final examination Robert Frost once gave to one of his classes. At the close of the course, the students gathered dutifully with their blue books, ball-points poised for three hours of question answering. Mr. Frost entered the room at the appointed hour and wrote the entire examination on the blackboard in two words: "Write something." Then he left.

For students not facile with pencil and paper, the teacher can turn to the dramatic arts. Drama, it seems to me, is perhaps the most powerful of all the arts in evoking existential awareness. In dramatic interpretation the pupil can literally assume the role of existential actor, making clear to himself—in the act of making something clear to his audience—what he considers the most important of his own subjective feelings. How one interprets a role inevitably reflects how one views his own life and its meaning in the world.

By way of an indirect example of such teaching, I have sometimes speculated on the appropriateness of an assignment like the following: The student in the eleventh-grade English class is asked to imagine himself a kind of benign Frankenstein (the college student might imagine himself a Watsonian Behaviorist psychological lab technician with a newborn baby assigned exclusively to him). The assignment is to write a description of the ideal human being that might be created, the individual with the finest set of attitudes, personality traits, life aspirations, and personal values. When the paper was turned in, the teacher would read it over and jot at the bottom of it a sequel assignment: "Now prepare a second paper in which you compare and contrast the individual you have created with yourself at this moment." This paper, in turn, would be submitted, the teacher would go over it, and the student would then be instructed to prepare and turn in a final, culminating assignment, namely, an explanation of why there was a discrepancy between the ideal and the actual individual since there is no excuse for not appropriating the attitudes, aspirations, values, etc., of the ideal individual as conceived. The point of the assignment would be to arouse disquiet in the student by showing him that he bears responsibility for falling short of his ideal goal.

Literature and the humanities

As Chapter 5 has emphasized, the Existentialist educator would seek to intensify the *normative* aspect of all subject matter. This is where personal judgment, in the manner of the Socratic pupil, can be exercised. The humanities obviously offer some of the most pregnant possibilities for such emphasis.

The conventional teaching of literature and the humanities assumes that literary documents, like natural phenomena in the sciences, lie outside the student's immediate life. They are to be studied and learned in the same way that one might study biology or mathematics, viz., to be comprehended as so much more verbal material concerning the world that lies beyond and independent of the learner. To look at the humanities in this way, the Existentialist educator might say, is to mutilate them and to destroy their most prominent contribution to human learning, namely, the awakening of sensibilities, the intensification of feelings in the individual.

To read the tales of Chaucer's pilgrims, to hear the lines of T. S. Eliot's "The Hollow Men," to study the essays of Ralph Waldo Emerson is *not* to be studying English. It is, rather, to be placing one's capacities for feeling at the disposal of an author who seeks to arouse feeling to a new, more intense level of awareness. To study literature is to lay bare the nerve endings of one's emotions and to invite stimulation from the author's work, much as the playgoer, upon entering the theater, deliberately opens his perceptive apparatus to receive symbolic experiences from the stage which will arouse new and hitherto unfelt emotions in his subjective consciousness. Consider any major theme of humanistic writing—death, love, suffering, guilt, freedom—and let the student in the classroom be put in touch with increasingly strong doses of what the important figures in our literary past have had to say about them. Of these, certainly the most powerful is the theme of death. Are we ready to induct high school youngsters into a subjective consideration of this most profound of human encounters? Are we prepared as teachers to have them really get inside this most existential of all human problems? The Existentialist teacher would insist on it. And he would introduce it to the youngster with materials ranging from Jack London's "To Build a Fire" to Caryl Chessman's *Cell 2455, Death Row*. Let the student get inside the heart of the man freezing to death, of the man before the firing squad or sitting in the electric chair or the gas chamber. Let him ponder the problem of capital punishment. Let him ponder the meaning of his own life by deliberately pondering the truth that on some future day it will be abruptly canceled from the universe with no trace remaining, as abruptly as any firing squad might cancel it.

History

The normative element subsides as we leave the arts and humanities and enter other subject matters which only partially lend themselves to Existentialist forms of teaching. History is a case in point because it can be taught in many different ways: as the chronological sequence of cause and effect through time, as the emergence and evolution of civilizations through the ages, as a series of heroic figures who have both shaped and been shaped by their times, or as an analysis of the ways in which human societies have solved their problems. These I think summarize the conventional "uses of the past," in Mueller's phrase. The Existentialist teacher of history would, however, find them all lacking. For one does not find the normative element in the study of history by viewing the past as something to be *used*. The past is not used; it is created. That is to say, what makes the past normative, expressive of the good-bad dimension of life, is not to be found in the past itself but in how we today view the past. It is our apprehension of what there is in history to value or reject which introduces the normative element into it. In this sense we *create* the value content of our heritage by viewing that heritage, and studying it, and teaching it to others in a particular light.

I realize that this conception of history, while enjoying some credence in historiographic circles, has only tenuous acceptance in American common sense. But it is essential to an Existentialist philosophy of historical education and is therefore worth some comment.

Kierkegaard used to say that you cannot learn from history until you have a life, an existence, of your own against which to judge history. History is no better a guide to behavior than contemporary society. For man cannot acquire moral and ethical principles from other men or other social institutions except by choosing them from the baseless platform of his own awareness of what is going on in contemporary life. He finds meaning in history only in terms of present circumstance.

There is no more appropriate way to exemplify this condition than to bear witness to American history itself. What does the United States Constitution say? What it says is plain enough; the Archives Building in Washington, D.C., still has the original. But what does it *mean*? This question cannot be answered except by living men. And the Supreme Court of this nation does not hesitate to interpret it for us, the living. The complaint is correct that in *interpreting* the Constitution this Court is actually *legislating*. And thanks for that! For if the Constitution were placed out of reach of living men, if they were barred from saying what it means in contemporary affairs, it would lose all significance as an historical document. Precisely because it is endowed with meaning *by the living* it remains a living document. Its meanings are authored in the here and now.

So it is with all of history. Past events may be said to exist in a brute, documentary, "archive" sense. But what they *mean* is always for us to say. The study of history is always an affair of the living present. Indeed, it is an affair of the future, of man's efforts to transcend his present situation in choosing his way forward to new and hitherto unexperienced spheres of awareness. Are we to say it is otherwise—that contemporary man is bludgeoned into certain views about his own past merely because that past *is* past and out of reach? What more insane and preposterous position could be taken? If we mean to be the masters of our fate, then certainly we must be the captains of our past. For a man to be "compelled" by history, he must freely *choose* to be compelled. He does not have to follow precedent. In the last analysis, he is the author of his own precedents. Only with this understanding can we regard the future as free and really at our disposal.

What we have said concerning a collective view of history can now be personalized in Kierkegaard's terms. Our own private sense of history, in the same fashion, originates in our private consciousness concerning the meaning of the past for ourselves. It is the epistemological notion of *appropriation*, discussed in the previous chapter, brought literally to bear on a commonplace subject matter of every school. Historical subject matter is to be appropriated, i.e., "made one's own," in the act of being learned. It must be opted for, adopted, and assimiliated into a private life before it can be considered knowledge in any scholastic sense.

To make history one's own and to make one's own history is to become involved in the interpretation of the past. It is to become personally implicated in the thrust and charge of events. It is to become emotionally a participant in the human enterprise. If we fought a Civil War, let each student feel the full voltage of that catastrophe; let him feel the exultation and heartbreak which that greatest of all national blunders burned into the American consciousness. Let him *feel* that war, as well as merely comprehend it as a 100-years-later bystanding spectator.

The above ideas find an apt summation in the following passage from Professor George Kneller:

> *History should be taught as a way to mold the future. There is no such thing as the "objectivity of history" because the objective world cannot finally be known, not, at least, alike to all men. The style and approach of a Mommsen or a Winston Churchill would be amenable to the existentialist. The latter, opinionated, prejudiced, in the eyes of the "objective historian," swings lustily into an interpretation of history which is his very own, once he has appropriated the content of his subject matter. The existentialist would hope for the fullest prior knowledge and understanding of history in all its proved facts, events, and detail; but he would urge that it be studied and written with Nietzschian anger and enthusiasm. The student should therefore learn to handle his history with passion, personal thrust, and in the manner of a stage director, talentedly manipulating the human scene, with all its heroes, villains, and plots.*[2]

Religion

Ever since America adopted secularism as a national ethic, the inclusion of religion in public education has been increasingly troublesome. The older, more traditional educational theories have generally held that religion is an essential ingredient in any educational program because the teaching of moral and spiritual values, unquestioned as an obligation of the school, was thought to be inextricably tied up with some theistic interpretation of life. Such values could not be taught in any other way.

An age of science, however, has convinced the American people that in improving the conditions of life reliance upon a supernatural deity is not an absolute necessity. Not only has the physical environment been effectively subdued and turned to man's account without any assistance from on high, but man's institutional structures and his very moral attitudes are now understood to be subject to his own thoughtful control. As a result, the American public school, under the influence of Experimentalistic science and Progressive principles, has gradually removed religious and mystical subject matters from the curriculum. The argument is that religious instruction is no longer necessary—indeed, is not even relevant—to the induction of the young into the American experience. Furthermore, such instruction divides and splinters the American polity because religious "knowledge" is of the sort which has no way of being either confirmed or refuted by any generally accepted method of inquiry. At any rate, in today's public schools, religious instruction is thought to have no place. Recent court decisions concerning prayer and Bible reading are final confirmations of this principle.

But, notwithstanding the court decisions and the inexorable triumph of scientistic secularism, there remains a strange inquietude in the American consciousness that something has gone wrong. There is something the matter with a society which refuses to acknowledge the public importance of religious curiosity. Certainly the most human of all questions is essentially a religious question: What is the meaning of my life? This is the question which religion has sought to answer. But merely because religion can answer it only in a variety of contentious and dogmatic ways, are we right in ignoring the question altogether, as our secular policy of exclusion maintains?

The Existentialist responds with a resounding "No," and he has something to say on the matter which, I think, can help us find our way out of this anomaly in American life. As we have seen in Chapter 2 (pages 32–38), all men share in the need for *recognition*, a need that is essentially religious in character. But let us remember that

The religious need is not necessarily a need to which there is a religious answer. It is simply the human need for ultimate recognition. The individual who knows he must die, . . . who cannot find the . . . over-all meaning that his being requires, wants above everything, some evidence that at least his need is recognized by others as the most important thing about him. He wants the universe itself to give some evidence, if possible, that it, too, recognizes this need as legitimate and appeasable. But there is no logical necessity which says that if there is a need for the universe to recognize and appease, the universe will oblige.[3]

Figure 2 visually explains our predicament. Here is the need for

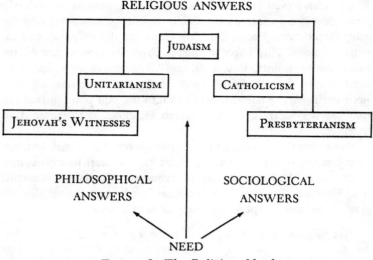

RELIGIOUS ANSWERS

FIGURE 2. *The Religious Need*

recognition. As we have seen earlier, men have tried to assuage it through recourse to philosophy and, more recently, social belonging. But one of their main attempts at finding solace has been in religion; they have sought answers to their need in the splintered sects of religious faith, in churches. They may have gone to the wrong place. It is not just a play on words to suggest that this is a case of misdirected faith.

The reason this area cannot be left to the churches is not because the churches do not deal with it adequately—which is true— or because most men are not touched by the churches; the reason is that this area does not belong to the churches; it belongs to all men. Existentialism serves both mankind and organized religion by extracting the very experiential base on which religion is founded and by calling it existential rather than religious.[4]

The existential need for recognition belongs to all men. And if education belongs to all men, then the school is obligated to pay attention to that need.

But at this point a tragic double error confounds contemporary educational theory: The traditional philosophies of education—

Idealism and Neo-Thomism—take their cue from organized religion and insist on introducing this or that religious answer into the school's program. They see such a course as the only way to deal with the need. This a secular society obviously cannot accept. But the Experimentalists, Positivists, and all shades of empirical secularists err on the other side! They refuse even to acknowledge the need itself, having talked themselves into the odd position that the only way to "deal" with it, in or out of school, is to ignore it altogether.

The Existentialist considers both policies hopelessly mistaken. His own position is not just a compromise but an effort to reclaim and to extract secular meaning from Everyman's existential predicament. The Existentialist grounds his position in adopting the religionist's *attitude* without adopting his many dogmatic answers:

> *The religious answer may seem to be a deceit and delusion, but its intention to answer something that must be dealt with because it is experienced is so much more honest and clearheaded than the attitude toward life of most of those [Experimentalists and Positivists] who waste time gibing against those who try to deal with something unquestionably serious.*[5]

We cannot ignore the quest for personal meaning. "No school has a right to be proud of its educational aims if it does not take into account this most important area of human experience and inquiry."[6]

How, then, does the Existentialist teacher instruct in this most existential of subject matters? Our solution turns out to be deceptively simple. If we refuse to ignore the need, and also refuse to offer answers to the need, what is left? The obvious alternative is to address ourselves and our students *to the need itself!* And here the Socratic paradigm comes to culminating relevance. The teacher's questions are absolutely without final answer: Just why do we have this need? What is the significance of this need in our lives? What importance, for you and for me, are we to attach to the quest for meaning, to the quest itself? In *questing* differently, do we therefore live differently, i.e., does it make a practical difference *how* one goes about the quest for meaning? Instead of pondering the existence of God, let us ponder *the need for a God.* Why do we feel we need him? This kind of discussion can effectively awaken the American youngster to that dimension of religious experience which is genuinely existential. Nor does this procedure violate the secular ethic; quite the contrary, the consideration of such questions completes the ethic by bringing that which is experienced by *all* men into the arena of open discourse. It fulfills, in an astonishingly apt way, the real meaning of a pluralistic society.

The Socratic dialogue, therefore, must be a part of the school's work.

THE PARADIGM SCHOOL

It is inevitable that we should want some clue as to whether such an education can really work—we are still pragmatists to that degree! Has anyone ever really organized a school designed to function on behalf only of the individual learner? As we all know, Progressive schools have often claimed this distinction, but I think in our latter-day assessment of their efforts we may conclude that they ultimately fell prey to the "socializing" theory of child development. They fostered the growth of individualism, but only in social terms, only in terms of the individual's relation to other members of the group or to the group itself.

Is there a school which has succeeded in holding "the others" at bay? A possible candidate is Summerhill, a small private school in England at Leiston, Suffolk, about 100 miles from London.[7] The school is now over forty years old, having been founded in 1921 by A. S. Neill, who has served as its original director but who is now over eighty and semi-retired.

For forty years "Neill," as his students call him, has been testing a hazardous hypothesis. Does freedom work? Suppose you had a school in which there were no rules, no requirements, no homework, no regulations, no roll taking, no grades, no academic expectations, no tests, no institutional code of decorum, no social conventions. Suppose all you had were a small "campus," some living quarters, some classrooms, half a dozen teachers, and forty to fifty youngsters ranging in age from five to seventeen. It would be a small but thoroughly free and open society, with no institutional "ethos" to adjust to and no organizational hierarchy to please. It would be, rather, merely a collection of separate individuals dealing with one another, old and young alike, as free and autonomous persons. Could anything like "education" possibly occur there? Neill has found that the answer is "Yes." And the story of his work is told with warmth and compelling dedication in the most recent and most famous of his many books, *Summerhill—A Radical Approach to Child Rearing.*[8]

The school draws its students from an admittedly atypical clientele. For one thing, there are tuition, boarding, and rooming fees; these run about $500 per year, a figure which is low compared with that at many other independent schools, but which nevertheless exerts a selective influence over admissions. For another, the school seems to attract many youngsters who have been in revolt against other kinds of schools, who have failed to adjust to institutional life, and who have been transferred by their parents to Summerhill. In the telling, Mr. Neill finds the greatest satisfaction in the rehabilitation of these youngsters. They come to Summerhill full of hate—for parents, for teachers and principals, for authority. Their previous encounter with learning has been so thoroughly associated with compulsory duties that they are at war not only with adult authority but with the very act of learning itself. They hate books, they hate study, they hate learning!

Their enrollment in Summerhill represents a traumatic and sudden "decompression" in the scholastic environment. All the pressures associated with "going to school" are abruptly lifted, and their customary response is precisely what one might expect—they play hooky, refuse to attend any classes or do any work; they indulge to the full their child impulses to play and play all day long. Neill lets them.

Sooner or later, though, they voluntarily take up their studies again. This interval Neill appropriately calls "recovery time"; it sometimes goes on for months. "The recovery time is proportionate to the hatred their last school gave them. Our record case was a girl from a convent. She loafed for three years. The average period of recovery from lesson aversion is three months."[9]

After the child is rehabilitated, he continues to be as free to determine his own routine and learning schedule as he was during his "recovery" period. He studies what he likes with the teachers he likes. He discovers himself in full responsibility for his own learning.

There is a timetable—but only for the teachers. The children have classes usually according to their age, but sometimes according to their interests. We have no new methods of teaching, because we do not consider that teaching in itself matters very much. Whether a school has or has not a special method for teaching long division is of no significance, for long division is of no importance except to those who want to learn it. And the child who wants to learn long division will learn it no matter how it is taught.[10]

What more apt way of stating the principle of "appropriation" implicit in Existentialist epistemology!

The school is also remarkable for its social freedom. The life of the community is in the hands of those who live in the community, the smallest child's vote exactly equal in strength to Neill's and to each teacher's. Punishment is meted out to individuals, not on grounds of having broken a school rule but rather on grounds that the culprit is interfering with the lives of others. If damage is done to school property, it is handled as a violation of Neill's private property and restitution must be made. If there is football in the lounge, it is treated as a disturbance of the peace and an invasion of others' rights of quiet and privacy. Even sex has no special containing bonds. Boys and girls are left alone, and relations between them appear to be healthy. Neill's approach to the matter exemplifies the only grounds for discipline, viz., infringing the freedoms of others: "I met them [two teen-age lovers] late one night and I stopped them. 'I don't know what you two are doing,' I said, 'and morally I don't care, for it isn't a moral question at all. But economically I do care. If you, Kate, have a kid, my school is ruined.' "[11]

There are rules, but only a few and those few reserved for palpable hazards: There is no swearing in town (permitted on campus), no running on the roof; no child may carry a gun or other weapon that can injure; and arson is automatically punishable. Except for these and a few others, all legislated by the self-governing General School Meeting of all Summerhill citizens, young and old, the life at this amazing institution is free, in both the "freedom from" and the "freedom to" sense of this word. As in any society, large and small, expectations and anticipations of others' behavior do develop. But at Summerhill the expectations are all person-to-person, I-Thou phenomena. The *institutional* is played down, the *personal* is played up. It is a close approximation of a society of *subjectivities*—free, autonomous, independent selfhoods, each determining the essence and meaning of his own life.

Neill has created a remarkable community on the basis of an exceedingly simple but powerful idea. He admits it has a lot of Freud in it: A free child is a happy child. A happy child does not fear or hate; he can love and give. The loving, giving child can live positively. Neill would be a more thoroughgoing exemplar of Existentialist education if he were to make one further, final argument which is implicit in his work: The free child eventually becomes the *responsible* child; it is freedom itself which makes this awareness possible. He who becomes responsible becomes capable of authenticity. Neill is creating authentic individuals.

Summerhill's graduates are proving out this thesis. Although there are some failures—some for whom a Summerhill education simply does not "take"—the preponderance of graduates are, in Neill's and society's terms, successes. They are living advertisements for the school: motion-picture cameramen, cooks and dietitians, ship's stewards, physicians, university professors, all of them self-directing and self-moving because they took charge of their own lives early and know what it means to be responsible for one's own career as a human being.

TEACHER AND STUDENT

We come at last to that electric arc, that tiny interhuman distance across which the final bolts of subjective energy must be thrown— the special relation that bears between the one who teaches and the one who learns. In the conventional psychology books this relation is always treated as a kind of natural phenomenon, much in the manner in which a biologist might consider the relation between the liver and the pancreas; it is thought of as an objective event in an objectively real world. Both teacher and pupil are turned into things. The psychologist watches them, trying to fathom the regularities of their behavior toward each other, then solemnly pronounces his "principles of teaching."

But in the end, the phenomenon of teaching and learning can never be fully understood in this way. The act of awakening awareness in another, of awakening freedom and responsibility there, cannot be "watched." It is an act which can be comprehended only by somehow being felt.

The paradigmatic Socrates was certainly interested in truth, but he was even more interested in *awakening another's awareness* of that truth. Even more, he was interested in awakening another's awareness of himself as a being-who-is-aware-of-truth, as a truth holder and a truth bearer. This was the whole point of his dictum "Know thyself." Kierkegaard once expressed a similar idea:

> If an Arab in the desert were suddenly to discover a spring in his tent, and so would always be able to have water in abundance, how fortunate he would consider himself—so too, when man who qua physical being is always turned towards the outside . . . finally turns inward and discovers that the source is within him.[12]

Earlier a distinction was drawn between Socrates of *The Meno* and Socrates of *The Republic*. In the book *Philosophical Fragments*—specifically in a section called "A Project of Thought"—Kierkegaard develops his understanding of this distinction as it relates to teacher and learner:

> If the Teacher serves as an occasion by means of which the learner is reminded, he cannot help the learner to recall that he [the learner] really knows the Truth; for the learner is in a state of Error. What the Teacher can give him occasion to remember is, that he is in Error. But in this consciousness the learner is excluded from the Truth even more decisively than before, when he lived in ignorance of his Error. In this manner the Teacher thrusts the learner away from him, precisely by serving as a reminder; only that the learner, in this being thrust back upon himself, does not discover that he knew the Truth already, but discovers his Error. . . . my own Error is something I can discover only by myself, since it is only when I have discovered it that it is discovered, even if the whole world knew of it before.[13]

Socrates' only claim to being wiser than his fellow citizens was the knowledge he had of his own ignorance (his Error). To be directly acquainted with one's own ignorance is a high form of wisdom. But it must always be private and solitary, since it is only when the individual has discovered his ignorance that it actually is discovered, even if the "whole world" and the teacher knew it before. The teacher's job in part then becomes one of awakening learners to themselves as learners and seekers and creators of their own truth from the starting place of the awareness of their own ignorance.

This kind of teaching obviously brings into play the more personal and intersubjective kinds of rapport. It is *not* to be confused with the pedagogical platitude about "being a pal to your students," or the cloying "Getting to Know You" song by the teacher, Anna, in *The King and I*. It is a deeper, more profound making of contact with another human being. Martin Buber has asked us to remember that "every human person born into this world represents something that has never existed before." The reality of the child is to be found in the fact that "In every hour the human race begins . . . in spite of everything, in this as in every hour, what has not been invades the structure of what is, with ten thousand countenances, of which not one has been seen before. . . ."[14] To make contact with the being of the learner is thus to make contact with that for which there is no precedent. Each encounter between teacher and learner therefore inevitably starts from scratch. It begins anew with a fresh creation still in the act of creating itself. The teacher's task is to see to it that this subjective selfhood, *de novo*, quickens its awarenesses of itself, of its freedom, and eventually of its responsibility for its own way of living a single human life.

The teacher's quest for awakening an awareness of freedom in the learner obviously requires a surrounding medium of freedom in the learning environment. This is the whole point of Neill's Summerhill, that the discovery of one's own subjective freedom can occur only in the freest possible learning circumstances. Moreover, freedom is the only medium in which the I-Thou relation can develop; it is the only vehicle in which genuine *communion*, in Buber's word, can be effected between teacher and learner.

Freedom is the vibrating needle, the fruitful zero. Compulsion in education means disunion, it means humiliation and rebelliousness. Communion in education is just communion, it means being opened up and drawn in. Freedom in education is the possibility of communion; it cannot be dispensed with and it cannot be made use of in itself; without it nothing succeeds, but neither does anything succeed by means of it: it is the run before the jump, the tuning of the violin, the confirmation of that primal and mighty potentiality which it cannot even begin to actualize.[15]

The policy of freedom has certain consequences we had better be prepared for. It means no hierarchy of authority in the school, no dominion of teacher over pupil, no external standards of achievement or success visited upon the young. It means that the students shall have not only a freedom *from* such standards but a coordinate freedom *to* establish their own standards in terms of which they choose to learn. But let them be mindful of the fact that they *are*, indeed, doing the choosing. The choices are theirs to be responsible for. When the full impact of their responsibility comes home to them, in that moment the need for tests and grades and report cards will have disappeared.

Finally, the teacher comes to realize that successful teaching in the Existentialist mode ends, as it began, in *paradox:* Such teaching succeeds by doing itself out of a job. It succeeds by becoming unnecessary, by producing an individual who no longer needs to be taught, who breaks loose and swings free of the teacher and becomes self-moving.

A teacher knows that he has succeeded only when he has evidence that his pupils can hold something to be true that he himself is convinced is true, without having come to this truth by imitating the teacher, by reasoning, or by other powers of persuasion, including the persuasion of example. When one sees one's own ideas quoted verbatim, one's heart should sink. But when one sees one's own ideas thought out anew as for the first time, then he is seeing the beginning of a free mind.[16]

And this is the heart of the paradox—that such teaching widens the distance between the teacher and the taught. "The good teacher aims to produce, not replicas, but men and women who stand apart from him even more distinctly than when he first met them."[17]

From the precarious establishment of "communion" the teacher creates an ever-widening distance. But the teacher knows that this distance is his greatest gift to his student. It is the distance that makes that student a mature self, a free, self-moving subjectivity. When that individual stands apart and alone, awake to his existing, aware of his freedom, responsible and in charge of his own life, he will see for himself why he may, for the first time, be called *authentic*.

NOTES

1. This is a good illustration of how we fabricate our own history without being aware of it. Socrates is seen and interpreted in terms of present-day categories and in terms of what a present-day "teacher" does.

2. George F. Kneller, *Existentialism and Education* (New York: Philosophical Library, 1958), pp. 129–130.

3. Ralph Harper, "Significance of Existence and Recognition for Education," chap. VII in N. B. Henry, ed., *Modern Philosophies and Education*, 54th Yearbook of the National Society for the Study of Education (Chicago: Published by the Society, 1955), p. 245.

4. *Ibid.*, p. 247.

5. *Ibid.*, p. 245.

6. *Ibid.*, p. 247.

7. The Summerhill Society with headquarters in New York City has imported the idea and now sponsors a similar school, founded in 1962, at present operating in Mileses, N.Y.

8. New York: Hart Publishing Company, 1960, 392 pp.

9. *Ibid.*, p. 5.

10. *Ibid.*

11. *Ibid.*, pp. 57–58.

12. From *The Journals*, reprinted in Robert Bretall, ed., *A Kierkegaard Anthology* (Princeton: Princeton University Press, 1951), p. 108.

13. From *Philosophical Fragments*, reprinted in Bretall, *op. cit.*, p. 158.

14. Martin Buber, *Between Man and Man*, trans. by R. G. Smith (Boston: Beacon Press, 1955; originally published in England, 1947), p. 83.

15. *Ibid.*, p. 91.

16. Harper, *op. cit.*, p. 237.

17. *Ibid.*

INDEX

157